Confessions of
an
Online Dating Addict

A True Account of Dating and Relating in the Internet Age

by

Jane Coloccia

authorHOUSE®

AuthorHouse™
1663 Liberty Drive, Suite 200
Bloomington, IN 47403
www.authorhouse.com
Phone: 1-800-839-8640

This book is a work of non-fiction. Unless otherwise noted, the author and the publisher make no explicit guarantees as to the accuracy of the information contained in this book and in some cases, names of people and places have been altered to protect their privacy.

First published by AuthorHouse 4/15/2008

ISBN: 978-1-4343-3204-2 (sc)
ISBN: 978-1-4343-3205-9 (hc)

Printed in the United States of America
Bloomington, Indiana

This book is printed on acid-free paper.

"I've been dating since I was fifteen. I'm exhausted. Where is he?"

Kristin Davis as Charlotte on *Sex and the City*

To everyone who wants to be loved,
and to those who must learn to love themselves, first.

Acknowledgements

This book would not have been possible had it not been for the support of so many people in my life.

First I would like to thank my parents, Anthony and Margaret, who always believed in me, supported me, and celebrated my ability to write. My Mom always knew I would "strike it big one day!" My sister, Sue, and her husband, Chris, were always there to provide a shoulder to cry on.

I promised a Lifespring trainer, Chris Lee, many years ago, when I wrote my book, I would dedicate it to him. This is not quite a dedication, but an important acknowledgement.

Thank you to Myla who told me I should take all my funny stories about online dating and write them down in a book. To Liz who got me started in online dating. And to my girlfriends Adele, Shelley, Ronni, Peg, Kerry, Pam, Vivian, Simone, and especially Bernadette, who would listen to all my horror stories about my dates.

Thank you to my friend, Monika, who agreed to help me market this book.

Thank you to my book editor, Elizabeth A. Grant (a.k.a. Beth) who lovingly took on this project and inspired me to make it the best it can be. She is at once a great editor, writer, and personal growth advisor.

Thank you to Jim Bitros who gave me the title for this book and Bruce Byers who shot my author photograph.

A very special thank you to Bernadette St. Pierre who not only told me to hold out for a man who was good enough for me, but who also proofread this book from cover to cover to make sure it was perfect. Immense gratitude also to her husband, the very talented Bill George of Synergy Arts, who designed a great cover.

Thank you to Clyde Baldo, my therapist and life coach, who kept pushing me to go for it and achieve my life's dream of publishing a book. He recounted a story to me about a client of his who was dabbling in acting. He suggested to this man "instead of just dipping your toe in the water, make a decision and step in all the way — or move on." This man chose to step in, as did I.

Thank you to my dog, Sophie, who put up with many a night when I typed away on my laptop instead of giving her belly rubs.

And finally, a huge thank you to Victor. For showing up. Caring about me. And getting me.

Table of Contents

Every Addiction Begins With A Beckoning — This Was Mine   1

The Online Virgin Has Her First Experience   5

I Dated Ronald McDonald   8

The Surfer Dude   12

The Stalker   15

The Artist   17

My British Fantasy   20

The Australian   25

The Phantom   27

The Younger Man   30

No Wills From New Jersey, Please!   34

Young Men With A Sense Of Humor   38

Guys Can Be Really Cruel   40

Some Men Just Want To Sweep You Off Your Feet   43

The Pothead   45

Instant Chemistry Addicts   50

The Lawyer   53

It Must Be The New Haircut And Glasses   56

Mr. Revenge   60

Unexpected One-Night Stands   63

A Couch Interlude   66

9-11 Strikes Too Close To Home   70

Dangerous Liaisons   82

Dangerous Liaisons Part Two   85

The New York State Trooper   88

The "Perfect" Guy   91

The Ferryboat Captain 96

Venturing Beyond My Comfort Zone 99

Trying To Get Over Myself 101

A Date With The Red Hat Society 112

Labor Day Romance 115

Even The Long Island Lolita Has A Profile 119

Do Celebrities Date Online? 121

The Princeton University Professor 123

The Real Estate Mogul 126

The Senior Citizen 128

The British Fantasy — Part Deux 131

Recycling A Relationship 136

The Dry Spell 148

Express Dating 150

And They Say Women Can't Make Up Their Minds! 153

When Worlds Collide 156

The Sports Writer 159

Some Dates Just Come Up Short 162

The Truth Hurts 164

The Flying Dutchman 167

Is It Time To Stop Dating Online? 171

When It Rains, It Pours 174

Life With Victor 178

And They Lived Happily Ever After? 181

Addendum

Sage Advice From A Woman Who Has Been There   189

Online Dating Protocol   190

Steer Clear Of Newbies   193

Be Prepared For Some Bizarre Experiences   195

Beware The Conquistadors   197

Really – It's Not Just Me   202

You Are What You Advertise   204

A Great Cure For Loneliness   206

The Profile   209

Kids ... Or No Kids? That Is The Question   211

Would I Do It Again?   214

A Professional Opinion   216

Every Addiction Begins
With A Beckoning
— This Was Mine

"Jane! I'm getting married!" Liz announced.

"Married?!" I exclaimed through the receiver. To *whom*? I wondered. I mean, I know I hadn't talked to Liz in awhile, but *married*? "Congratulations!" I said.

Turns out his name was Lou — and she had met him *online*! Just the thought of it made me cringe. (And shudder. Sort of a crudder.)

Liz had been dating a toxic loser for what seemed like forever (she called him "The Albatross") and she told me the prior New Year's Eve, she'd promised herself she would never spend another New Year's alone. So, she decided to get into the online dating game. She met exactly 10 men on her online adventure. Evidently number 10 was "the one." Lou was about her age (late forties), divorced, and interested in settling down. They became engaged only four months after their cyber introduction.

With this one bit of news, my whole world changed. Perhaps online dating *wasn't* just for losers. After all, Liz was a sane, successful businesswoman. The way she put it, it's all a numbers game. Online dating simply means you're widening your net, she explained, meeting more men in hopes of finding your soul mate — or the one man you really click with. It made perfect sense.

Since I had been spending most of my nights alone and hadn't been asked out on a date in, oh, about a million years, I figured I had nothing to lose. As soon as I signed up and started "searching," I was like a kid in a candy store. Here were men of all shapes and sizes: blondes, brunettes, redheads, from all backgrounds and all types of careers. Gobs and gobs of men! It was almost too good to be true.

Little did I know this online dating thing would quickly become almost a full-time job. Once I had my photo and profile posted, I would wake up each morning to at least 50 e-mail inquiries from men, with an additional 50 or so throughout the day. Do the math, people! That is 700 inquiries being showered upon me a week. I felt like I needed a secretary just to keep up with it all.

At the time, even with all of these prospects, I was hesitant to actually meet anyone in person. I figured I would do the e-mail and instant message thing for a while until I felt more comfortable — or got up the guts — to actually meet someone in the flesh, so to speak. But much to my dismay, I learned my standoffishness was a turnoff. I was quickly losing admirers! You have no idea the blow I took when my sea went from 20 good fish a day to a mere 16!

Okay, I'll admit it. Perhaps the reason I was a bit hesitant about meeting people was because while my headshot was rather attractive, I'd been packing on some extra pounds below the belt.

I guess I also liked the game-playing aspect of cyber communication. I discovered previously hidden talents, for instance. Like I was great at giving phone and e-mail. Men loved talking to me and writing back and forth. Plus, on the phone or via instant messaging, I could be a perfect version of me. I didn't have to worry about if my butt was too big. In fact, I could sit there in the comfort of my own home in my pajamas on a Sunday afternoon and have amazing conversations with perfectly eligible men without even having to wash my face or comb my hair.

But sooner or later, the jig was up! I had to agree to meet or risk losing potential Prince Charmings. Granted, there were some guys who were into IM-ing forever, but not many, and at some point, I had to wonder, "Is that really the behavior of a highly desirable man, or is he just some big-butted unshaven pajama-wearing cad?"

Alas, it is addictive. It's rather nice, you see, to open your e-mail each morning to find dozens of messages from guys telling you how pretty you are and how they'd love to meet you.

The constant contact seduced me long before I met someone face-to-face. For a while, it began to take over my life. I never wanted to be too far from my computer, craving the attention from new admirers. I was online morning, noon, and night. It was becoming ridiculous. I suppose it was a way to feed the loneliness and actually feel like I was doing something about my situation. But eventually, reality kicked in, and I remembered about actually wanting to meet someone and get married. And I was pretty sure it would require an in-person meeting.

I've never had a lot of luck being asked out in the non-cyber world. There seems to be something about my persona that intimidates men. It's like a subliminal signal I must give off. I think part of the problem is I own my own public relations and marketing consulting business. Men don't know what to make of me. They figure, I don't need them to support me, so why *do* I really need them? And for many men, the fact I make more money than they do seems to be intimidating.

Or perhaps, if I seem untouchable or aloof, then maybe, too, I don't have to worry about being rejected. It's easier not to let someone get close in the first place, right? Unfortunately, that doesn't work if you actually want to be in a relationship. It was time to let my guard down and dip my toe in the water.

The Online Virgin
Has Her First Experience

One of my first admirers was the Greek scientist.

We were chatting on the phone early one Sunday afternoon, swapping our online dating stories, since I was fairly new to the game. He seemed like a nice enough guy. He invited me to dinner, but I hesitated, making excuses and saying I didn't really know him that well yet. His manner was quiet and comforting, and he convinced me I could be scared and stay in my apartment or I could take a chance and come out and meet someone. And so I agreed.

We met at his favorite Greek restaurant not far from my apartment in Manhattan. It was late afternoon and the sun was starting to go down. He met me at the bar and then guided me to a table outside. I thought it was a bit odd that he was wearing sunglasses indoors, but I brushed it off.

He didn't really smile, and as it got darker and darker, I kept waiting for him to take off his sunglasses, but they remained on.

As dinner progressed, he was very self-absorbed and talked a lot about his career and what he had to offer a woman. He also remarked he didn't think we had made a connection and didn't feel any chemistry.

"It's rather hard to make any kind of a connection with a person when you can't see their eyes," I said. "And it's rather rude." He relented. Unfortunately, there wasn't much behind the lenses. His eyes weren't very expressive and I guess in hindsight it was his way of hiding.

Needless to say there was no love match, but I had done it. I'd had my first online dating experience! And it wasn't horrible, so I was ready to get out there and try again.

I should mention I was never a big dater. For some reason I was *never* asked out in high school, and while I had my crushes on guys, they were always interested in dating someone else. I never even went to the prom, and once in college, I still never had a boyfriend. That definitely does a number on a girl's self-confidence! Here I had friends who were quite popular, and yet I spent my time telling my diary how heartbroken I was or how a guy failed to notice me, or who was taking so-and-so to the prom.

In fact, I didn't even date very much in my twenties. Part of the reason was I was busy trying to establish myself in my career, first working for other people, and then starting my own business at the age of 27. Over time, I developed a fear of intimacy. What if I let someone get too close? Would they like the real me?

In my twenties and early thirties I did date a bit — but not a lot. Who knows? Maybe I really did exude some vibe that said "don't come near me," because I rarely got asked out. I also didn't really drink and hated hanging out in smoky bars. So where was I going to meet a man? I worked in an industry where most of the men were gay — or the few straight ones were already married. So I would spend many a Saturday night sitting at home watching television — and believe it or not — Prince Charming never came riding on his white horse into my living room on the 29th floor.

Online dating was an incredible opportunity for me, because I finally felt in control. Here I could put myself in an arena where the sole focus was to meet men and hopefully develop a relationship. And I could be aggressive, take the first step, and ask a guy out — and it was perfectly acceptable! I might not have understood why a man would wear sunglasses indoors, but there was one thing I was sure about: online dating was like nothing I had ever experienced before!

I Dated Ronald McDonald

A few months into my adventure, I met Dick.

"You seem like a very lovely person – the kind of person that I would really like to get to know better."

"From your photos I can tell that your kind eyes and your warm smile will melt the heart of many a guy. You seem like a genuine and graceful woman. I am also intrigued that you are a writer and would love to learn more."

"I am online searching for my soul mate. A woman whom I can love and treasure and with whom I can create a truly safe space to nurture and grow together."

With e-mails like this, soon I felt comfortable enough to move on to phone chats.

The first time we talked on the phone, I found myself exhausted. It was like talking to the Energizer Bunny. Dick was so "wired"! He never shut up, and I thought, "Okay, maybe this guy isn't for me." He kept up his side of the conversation so well I barely had to "uh-huh" and "yeah" for him every now and again. I mean, I could have taken a shower and gotten dressed during our call and he wouldn't have even known I was gone. After awhile, I ended the call simply because it was so draining keeping up with him. But I chalked it up to nervousness and decided to give the guy a break.

Dick called again a few nights later and invited me to dinner.

"Um, to be honest, Dick, I feel a bit uncomfortable going out with someone who won't tell me what they do," I said.

"What does that really matter?" he said. "It's nothing illegal, I promise."

"I would just feel better if I knew what it was."

"Jane, I would tell you if I could, but it's confidential and I am not allowed to tell anyone," he said.

"Do you work for the CIA or something?" I said.

Laughing, he said, "No. It's not anything so mysterious."

"Well, if you don't tell me, then I'm sorry, but we're not going to meet."

Silence. More silence. It was difficult to do, but I waited it out and stood my ground. Finally, he relented.

"Okay, Jane. I will tell you what I do, but you can *never* tell anyone."

"Okay ..." I said, wondering for a moment if I really wanted to know the answer.

"I am an actor," he said.

"Well, that's not so bad," I thought.

"I play Ronald McDonald actually," he said. "I go around to elementary schools performing as Ronald in skits about diversity and recycling and things like that. I'm not allowed to tell anyone because people are supposed to think there is just one Ronald, but in actuality, there are five of us here in the tri-state area."

To be honest, I was rather dumbfounded. Here I was thinking he did something sinister or really top secret and his job couldn't have been more harmless.

During our next conversation to finalize dinner plans, he seemed a little saner. "Does it freak you out that I'm Ronald McDonald?" he asked.

"It's a bit strange," I said. "But I understand why you do it." Hey, he was an actor in New York City who needed to make a buck, so I couldn't blame him.

Dick lived in Greenwich Village and since I had to go pick up a movie poster I was having framed down there, we decided to meet at the poster store and take it from there. He was tall and lanky, had nice blue eyes, and looked like a more rugged Keith Urban. Much to my dismay, the poster turned out to be much bigger and heavier than I expected, and Dick graciously offered to take it back to his apartment for safekeeping while we had dinner. So we walked to his apartment, and I waited outside while he took it upstairs.

We ate at a nice Italian place in the Village and had a great time. He told me he was divorced, had two kids and made quite a nice living playing Ronald. There was a part of me that still didn't believe him, and so after dinner, we strolled through the Village and with the aid of enough red wine, I convinced Dick to let me come back to his apartment to check out the outfit.

He lived in a three-story walk-up and as we climbed to each floor, I really couldn't imagine what I was about to find. He opened the door to a very spacious apartment with exposed brick and he offered me something to drink. "The heck with the drink," I thought. I wanted to see the getup! After some cajoling and flirting, he walked over to the closet and there it was … the red wig, yellow overalls, and, yes, big clown shoes.

"You really need to see it on me with the white face makeup," Dick commented.

There was no hiding it; I was in the presence of an honest-to-goodness Ronald McDonald.

Dick had a soft and compassionate side I found attractive. On our second date, we went back to his apartment, and as he was telling me about his divorce, he began sobbing uncontrollably. He confessed he was bi-polar, on medication, and went from high-highs (like the night he was chatting on the phone with me) to low-lows when he was so depressed he could barely get himself out of bed.

I soon realized Dick was in no shape for any type of commitment (although maybe I should reconsider that statement), and we went our separate ways.

There was a McDonalds about one block away from the apartment where I lived at the time, and it had one of those plastic life-size Ronald McDonald figurines sitting on a bench with his leg crossed and his arm out so people could sit and pose with him for a photo. Every time I walked by that statue I just smiled and laughed. If only people really knew.

The Surfer Dude

One day, I was online and found Tim. He was from Los Angeles and drop-dead gorgeous.

Not having much self-esteem at the time, I usually didn't e-mail guys who I thought were incredibly handsome. I knew I wouldn't have a chance with them. But day after day, seeing Tim online, I couldn't take it anymore, and figured, "What the hell, I'll say hi. The worst he can say is 'no thanks.'"

Tim and I started communicating back and forth quite a lot. He was very down-to-earth and cool and I don't think he had a clue how cute he was, which made him all the more attractive. He had just moved to the New York area and was working at a new job in IT.

After weeks and weeks of instant messaging and e-mailing, we finally decided to meet for lunch one Sunday afternoon. Much to my surprise, he wasn't as much of a god as I had initially thought, although he was still quite cute. (Evidently he photographed well.)

"So what's your story, Tim?" I said. "How come a cutie like you is single?"

Smiling, he responded, "Well, I was married. My wife was a producer for *Entertainment Tonight*. One day I came home from work to find her in bed with another guy."

"Oh my God! I'm so sorry," I said.

"Yeah, it was kind of surprising," he said. His smile faded and his eyes began welling up with tears. "Apparently it happens a lot in Hollywood. She didn't seem to think it was a big deal. I tried to stay and work it out. But I just couldn't trust her and was always wondering where she was and who she was with."

As he spoke, tears began streaming down his face and I could tell the wound was still quite raw. I think he chose to move across the country to get away from his situation, but as they say, "Wherever you go, there you are," so I don't think his change of address really helped the situation. It was clear — yet once again — he was in no shape for a relationship.

One thing I need to interject here is that in my experience with meeting men through online dating, I came across many, many men who had been wronged by women. Before that, I had a very stereotypical attitude, thinking men primarily cheated on women. But after meeting a lot of men online who had been cheated on, I've completely changed this opinion. And in many cases, it seemed they weren't able to get over it.

Tim and I met one other time a month or so later and went to a movie. He was still quite sad and clearly looking for nothing more than a friend. Every once in a while we would e-mail and check in with one another. I think at one point, he was considering going back to California because he and his surfer-style sports car didn't much like winter on the East Coast.

I hope by now he's over his ex-wife. He was a nice guy who deserved to be happy.

The Stalker

People warn us about online dating for good reason.

While nine out of 10 people online are probably normal, there are those sick, scary individuals whom you want to stay as far away from as possible. Peter was one such guy.

I remember getting an e-mail from him asking me to check out his profile. I looked at it and he was much older than I was and I didn't find him attractive, appealing, or thought we had anything in common. So I replied very nicely that I didn't think we were a match and I wished him the best of luck.

But this guy wouldn't take no for an answer! He kept contacting me and telling me he had posted new photos or asking me to instant message with him and get to know one another better.

At one point — I don't know how he did it — he actually figured out my AOL address and was sending me e-mails and instant messages constantly. Every time I logged on, there he'd be. "Stop playing hard to get," he'd say. "I like a challenge, so keep it up," he'd say. I kept trying to block him and he kept getting through. After awhile, it became sick. He would tell me I was a nasty shrew and it was his mission on this earth to tame me and make me fall in love with him.

Thankfully, all of this took place "virtually," and he never got my phone number or address, but it was indeed a scary experience.

Another man e-mailed me from Florida. He had this really long, gross hair, no teeth, and was unemployed. I told him very nicely I didn't think we were a match and I wished him the best of luck.

He wrote back and told me he had printed out my photo and masturbated to it every night.

The Artist

After the usual e-mail exchange, I agreed to meet "The Artist" for dinner.

He was a painter and a good one at that. He showed me photographs of his work, and I have to say I was really impressed. It was a style that appealed to me — perhaps more so than the artist itself.

He was a nice enough guy — blonde, blue-eyed, and slim — quite attractive, really. He showed up for dinner at a little bistro on the corner of 29th Street wearing a blue blazer and jeans. His profile listed his age as 39. (As it turns out, I think he was closer to 49.) He was very Bohemian, had lived in Europe for quite some time and had a son with a woman there. I couldn't tell if he had any interest in me or not until he walked me home, and as we were saying goodbye, he thrust his tongue down my throat. Fast guy. Way too fast.

While I knew I wasn't really interested in dating him, the public relations/marketing part of me was interested in helping him. I knew a gallery owner in SoHo and set up a meeting for him at 2 p.m. the following Sunday.

The Artist had an unusual lifestyle, but I suppose maybe not for an artist, on second thought. He painted all night and slept most of the day, and sold his work on a street corner in SoHo on weekends. He told me to give him a call at noon on Sunday to make sure he was awake. When I did, it was clear I had woken him up.

"Will you come by and pick me up?" he said, his voice still raspy with sleep. I hesitated. "And by the way, bring me a cappuccino, a pack of Marlboros, and a tuna fish sandwich, okay?"

I stopped at the deli on the street around the corner from his apartment and picked up the requisite items and then headed up to his apartment — on the fifth floor of a five-story walkup. By the time I got to the top of the stairs, I was heaving for oxygen. He opened the door buck-naked. I did my darnedest not to drop my eyes below his chin.

"Come in. Make yourself comfortable," he said. (Kind of tough given his state of undress.) "I'll just take a quick shower."

I walked into his shoebox of a living room and looked around in complete horror. There was exactly one floor tile free where I could stand. There were painting materials, clothing, magazines, newspapers, and just plain junk piled up everywhere. He said he had been in the same apartment for 29 years — and I believed him! This was one of those places where they find the inhabitant dead and rotting after no one has seen him for months. I could see why he hadn't moved. The thought of having to sift through all the junk was simply overwhelming. And so I stood on my little floor tile and waited until he came out of the shower — still naked.

He walked back into the living room, eating his tuna sandwich and dressing at the same time. He grabbed a pair of pants off the floor — yes, he went commando — and a T-shirt, and off we went. During the 10-minute taxi ride from his apartment to the gallery, I saw a side of him I couldn't believe. He berated the cab driver so mercilessly about his driving, the driver pulled over and ordered us out of the cab. Never, in my life, have I ever been thrown out of a taxi! I was mortified to say the least.

Then, at the gallery, he launched into a raucous debate about art versus the establishment rather than trying to sell the gallery owners on his work. Despite his outburst, they still expressed interest in his work and asked him to have some of his canvases delivered to the gallery the following week. Even before we left the gallery, I knew he wouldn't bother to follow-up.

After the meeting, we walked to the corner in SoHo where his friend was minding the street corner where he displayed his art, and I just stood there as he downplayed the meeting to his friend — a fellow painter.

It seemed The Artist didn't really want to be anything more than a painter who sold his work on a street corner in Manhattan.

My British Fantasy

Every American girl has fantasies about dating a British guy.

We love that accent, and they always come across so smooth and intelligent, whether they really are or not. A Masterpiece Theater – PBS — Hugh Grant type of guy.

I don't quite recall whether Colin contacted me first or I him, but it quickly elevated into quite a "romantic relationship" before we had even met. We e-mailed quite a lot and even "broke up" on e-mail at one point. Yes, this is really possible.

He was a sales and marketing vice president for a company in Connecticut, and had been in the U.S. for a few years pursuing the American dream. He had two kids whom he left back in England with their mother (whom he had never married); however, he seemed more proud of the fact he drove a Porsche and was living near the water than that he was a father.

As so often happens in online dating — at least in my case anyway — Colin and I chatted for hours on the phone. We both had hectic travel schedules. He would call me constantly or send e-mails all day long. While he was at a sales conference, he kept walking out of the meeting to call me and say hello.

"Darling, I can't go a minute without thinking of you," he would say. Realize, I had still never met the guy! Evidently our cyber/phone relationship was starting to affect his work, because he was either e-mailing me or IM-ing me or calling me constantly. Even the people he worked with were starting to wonder about him — and he said it became difficult for him to talk with me and then to go back into the meeting because invariably he would always develop a "stiffie."

As soon as he got back into town, I had to head to London on a business trip. I arrived at the Mandarin Oriental Hotel and was escorted to my room by the front desk clerk. I was definitely jet-lagged and wasn't really paying complete attention to her, but as we entered my suite, I did notice she was smiling intently. "That's odd," I thought. And then she walked me into the bedroom.

"Your boyfriend must really love you," she said.

At first I hadn't a clue what she was talking about. Let's see, she had remarked my boyfriend must really love me, but last I checked, I didn't have one. Then I noticed this enormous teddy bear from Harrod's propped atop the bed with a card. She was grinning from ear to ear, and I just stood there in shock wondering who the heck this teddy bear could be from.

When I opened the card, it said "Welcome to London! Have a nice stay. — Colin."

I couldn't believe it! Not only had he arranged for me to have a gift in my room, but he had arranged for the biggest darned teddy bear I had ever seen in my life. That bear — off white and with a gold silk Harrod's ribbon on it — had to be at least three feet tall!

During the rest of my time there, Colin would call constantly and we would talk for hours, which must have cost him a small fortune. I even called him one time using my calling card and when I got home found I had racked up a phone bill in excess of $150! Oops.

At one point during our phone conversations, Colin mentioned he was already trying to figure out how he was going to ask my father for my hand in marriage. Yes, I know this sounds ridiculous! But it was romantic. I was in London, being courted by a British guy in America, and he was telling me he was falling in love with me and thought we were going to get married! What girl wouldn't be smitten — you couldn't write a Hollywood blockbuster better than this.

For all of you non-online daters, I know this seems totally unimaginable. How can you have feelings for someone whom you have never met? But two people can create a very deep sense of intimacy — however false — from verbal and written communication. And yes, men who've never met you can get "stiffies" just from the sound of your voice. That's all I can say.

When we finally met, I had to admit he didn't look much like his picture, which was a cross between Hugh Laurie and Ralph Fiennes. The reality was more along the lines of a young John Cleese. But of course, with all of the sexual tension built up from weeks of conversation, we soon found ourselves in bed. Afterward, we lay there and he seemed distant.

"What are you thinking about?" I asked.

"I'm thinking of buying a boat. I was just trying to figure out how much to offer," he said. A rather odd statement considering the moment, and a complete turnoff, I might add.

After awhile, we got ourselves dressed and decided to go out. Since it was nearly Christmas, I took him to Rockefeller Center to see the tree. He was more excited because he knew there was a Tourneau store in Rockefeller Center and he could go look at Rolex watches. I waited for nearly an hour while he talked with the salesman about the latest Rolex watch (which evidently was better than the one on his wrist).

Later that day, we hung out in the bar at the New York Palace hotel and then had dinner at the Monkey Bar, a legendary Manhattan restaurant. He had brought an overnight bag. See, the plan was for him to stay over and spend the weekend at my place. But after dinner, he told me he wanted to go home.

"You're all right, huh, darling?" he said. "I just have some things I need to take care of."

My gut told me something was fishy. "Okay," I said.

"I'll ring you tomorrow," he said, and took off in his Porsche.

When I hadn't heard anything by mid-afternoon — this from the man who would call me constantly every day and night — I called him. He seemed quiet and distant.

"What's up, Colin?" I said. There was a long pause.

"Well, I don't know how to say this. You see, I was a bit shocked yesterday when we finally met. It's quite upsetting. There just doesn't seem to be any chemistry between us," he said.

Hey mate, chum, or whatever you Brits call your friends, there was enough something there yesterday for you to sleep with me! Or was it just a practice run, a litmus test?

But no, he went on about he was just very disappointed and disheartened and he didn't know what to do. And that was the last I heard from Colin.

As for the big teddy bear from Harrod's, I failed to mention what a nightmare it was to bring home. The concierge at the Mandarin Oriental — who it turns out had secured the bear in the first place — had tossed out the original packaging. So I ended up just tucking the bear under my arm and carrying him to the airport in London. I have to say, I have never seen anything elicit so many smiles and stares from people in my life. Here was a grown woman carrying a teddy bear through Heathrow Airport just weeks before Christmas. I'm sure they were imagining me bringing it home to a waiting child. Little did they know it was from my online lover!

I was hoping for an empty seat in which my new friend could ride, but the flight home was sold out, so I had to stuff him in the overhead compartment — no small task, let me tell you. He then took up residence on the living room chair in my apartment.

Once Colin gave me the kiss-off, I couldn't bear to look at the creature any longer, so I ended up donating him to my office's Toys for Tots collection. Everyone thought I was so generous to donate such a great gift. In reality, I just couldn't wait to be rid of it and the memory of Colin.

In hindsight, I must say I was more attracted to the romantic notion of dating a Brit than the reality of it. He was incredibly materialistic and we didn't share any values. But when you are dating and desperate, a romantic fantasy — and an afternoon of sex — does come in handy.

The Australian

Every online dater eventually comes across a person who positively knocks your socks off by their photo.

And I don't know about other people, but when someone is more gorgeous than I am, I tend to have self-confidence issues. But there are the days when you do think, "Oh, what the hell!"

The Australian was gorgeous — in his mid-forties, a successful businessman, a cross between Clive Owen and Rob Lowe, and he agreed to meet for a drink. Hey, it was a plus.

We planned to meet at the bar in The Waldorf=Astoria, and when we arrived, it was so crowded, there wasn't any place to sit or talk where we could hear one another. I remembered the Greek restaurant nearby where Mr. Sunglasses had taken me and I suggested we go there.

He wore all black and was a vision to the eyes. We sat at the bar and talked. After awhile, I turned to him and said, "Well, how do you think it's going?"

He turned to me and said, "I like you. You're really cute. Let's do this again."

As I walked home, I was filled with excitement and anticipation. Finally, my dream hunk! Here I was, recounting the conversations we had in my head and wondering what we would do on our next date. He had told me about some of his favorite restaurants, what he liked to do for fun, places he wanted to see and travel. This was my most romantic fantasy come to life.

I never heard from him again.

I tried to reach him a few times, but I either got his voice mail, or he would say he was in a meeting or running somewhere and would get back to me. And then he just faded away, which is evidently exactly what he intended to do.

You come to learn this happens a lot with online dating, even more so than when your first encounter with a person is face-to-face. When online guys aren't interested, they just disappear rather than being honest and telling you, "I'm just not that into you."

The Phantom

Mac and I made a connection through a site called Matchmaker. com. I'm not even sure it exists anymore.

We sent e-mails back and forth through the site for quite some time, and then we exchanged regular e-mails and began IM-ing. We seemed to really hit it off, and yet I had never seen his photo. During the time we had first started corresponding, he told me he was in San Francisco on a business trip and would be there for a few weeks, so the best he could offer was e-mail.

And so our e-mail relationship began — day and night. I don't quite remember what he did — perhaps an investment banker — but we got to know one another quite well, and then, as sometimes happens, our e-mails became a bit raunchy and I suppose two lonely individuals communicating online late at night were looking to make a connection.

"Dear Jane, I am sitting here in my hotel room in San Francisco thinking about what I would do if we were together and I was

coming home to you. We could order in some Chinese, watch a bit of television, and then go to bed early because, after all, I've been out of town all week. I would take a shower to wash the travel grime off of me — and maybe you even want to join me. Then afterwards, we could towel one another off and enjoy some long lingering kisses before I picked you up and brought you into our bedroom ..."

After awhile, however, his communication became all about sex. Not so much as a "How was your day?" before diving right in. That got old really fast for me, so I broke it off.

A week or so later, Mac was back, e-mailing me, and apologizing. I must admit, I had really gotten used to the attention, so it began again. But our correspondence rapidly deteriorated into the sexual genre again and I kept asking when we would meet. He was either really busy at work or traveling all the time. Perhaps that should have been my first clue.

"Can we at least talk on the phone?" I asked.

"I'm having awful problems with my cell phone service," he would say. "As soon as I get back to New York, I'll take care of it. Be patient, okay?"

"I suppose," I would say, "but this e-mailing is getting really old." Yet, at the same time, the attention and predictability of it became addictive. When you're lonely and haven't been in a relationship in awhile, just hearing anybody tell you they miss you can be comforting.

Even so, I kept the pressure on about wanting to talk and meet. On my birthday, I came into my office to find a message from him on my voice mail wishing me a happy birthday. It really made my day! He had a Southern drawl — not at all what I had expected — but he didn't leave a call back number, nor did my company's phone system have caller ID. Drats!

Unfortunately happy birthday would have to be it. Mac never called again. He e-mailed quite a lot, but after a time I grew weary of the entire exchange. Now that I think back on it, I am sure he was probably married or somehow unavailable. Silly me — I thought people on dating sites were actually interested in *dating*; maybe even creating a relationship. But I have learned people are looking to make all types of connections — some if only just virtual.

The Younger Man

When I began dating online, I didn't really have much use for younger men. In fact, I was never even attracted to them.

I was of the opinion men were pretty much less mature at equal ages with women anyway, so dating a man my age or younger probably wasn't such a good idea. And I had always seen myself with an older guy anyway — just not one eligible for Medicare!

So one day I got a "wink" from Larry, which is an indicator you can use on the sites to express possible interest. He was eight years younger than me and looked a lot like Vince Vaughn. Larry kept inviting me out and I kept bluntly telling him I had no use for a younger man. But he was quite persistent and really wouldn't let up, begging me to give him a chance. He had a pretty good sense of humor and I gave him points for tenacity. So finally, I gave in.

He arranged to take me to dinner at a very upscale New York City restaurant — one that was rated among the top 10 in the city by the Zagat guide. Larry had style!

We met at the restaurant and he was quite well dressed — in a suit — and we had a nice dinner, although I could tell he was very nervous. Youth. Maybe it is nerve-wracking going out with an older woman. It certainly wasn't with a younger man. Later in the evening, he told me he was so attracted to me when I walked in the door he actually had "a boner" as we walked to the table.

On our second date, he invited me to dinner and a movie and we had a nice time. About midway through the movie, he nervously grabbed my hand to hold, which I thought was pretty cute.

Larry was fun. I wasn't overly interested in or attracted to him, but instead was in the mode of, "Hey, this is a man and he is interested in me."

Oh, before I forget, the week before Larry and I met face-to-face, he told me he was mugged. He wanted to warn me he had some black and blue marks on his face. But back to the story.

After we were dating for a few weeks, we made plans to get together on Saturday evening (he lived way out on Long Island in Southampton). But as the week wore on, I never heard from him. I kept calling and calling, but he never answered his cell phone. He had also given me a number for a house he was renting in Southampton as well as the phone number for his parents' house, where he sometimes stayed as well.

So the entire weekend went by with no phone call. Finally I heard from him on Monday.

"Jane, I'm sorry I didn't call. I was in a bad accident. My Jeep was rear-ended on the Long Island Expressway and I was in the hospital all weekend. I kept saying to the nurses, 'Jane, Jane ... I have to call Jane,' but I was very confused, because I was knocked out for quite a long time."

"Oh my God," I said. "Are you okay?"

He told me he was out of the hospital, but housebound, healing from his wounds. Apparently he'd had a concussion and some broken ribs. So the plan was for me to go out to Southampton that following weekend to visit him. I checked my Southampton Jitney bus schedules and got myself all packed. We agreed to touch base on Friday afternoon so I could tell him what bus I'd be on so someone could pick me up.

Friday came. I called and called, but again, he didn't answer his cell phone. I called his parents' house and left a message with his father, who informed me he hadn't seen him. By Saturday afternoon, I still hadn't heard from him and began to worry. I called his parents house again and finally in the early evening, his mother answered the phone.

"Have you seen Larry?" I asked. "I was supposed to get together with him yesterday and haven't been able to get a hold of him."

"No," she said. Something struck me as funny about her response. I mean, that's it, just "No"?

"Aren't you worried he's been sick and you haven't seen him and no one can reach him?" I asked.

"No, dear," she responds. "Don't worry about him .... he doesn't worry about anyone else and all is not as it seems," she said, and she hung up.

I stood there in shock. Didn't she care at all about her son?

About a week later, I finally got a hold of Larry at his office. His manner was completely nonchalant. It was as if he hadn't left me hanging all weekend. But, stupid, desperate me, I went back for more. "So when am I going to see you again?" I asked. (Boy, this is starting to become a pattern, huh?)

He began with the excuses again, and I notice his voice sounded very strained.

"My brothers are trying to force me out of the family business," he tells me. "I really need to concentrate on this now. I don't know what to do."

Oh, the drama. I couldn't believe how much drama surrounded this guy — the mugging, the car accident, the family business troubles. (Believe it or not, there was more, but it would take a whole book to fill you in.)

Was it all true? Who knows. Finally, I just had to let it go. It was amazing to me how someone who could be in such hot pursuit of me could suddenly turn so cold. Maybe like they say — whoever "they" are — for many guys, it's all about the chase.

No Wills From New Jersey, Please!

Prior to my online dating escapades, I had a relationship with a man named Will from New Jersey.

It ended disastrously — probably due to the fact he was married and lied about it. So in my early online dating adventures, I met another guy named Will from New Jersey, and from these two facets of his profile alone, I was already wary. It was also during a time when I was having extra bad luck in online dating and was a bit gun-shy.

I remember telling Will how I had been burned and was afraid to take a chance again and he said, "Don't worry, I won't hurt you."

So we met one night for dinner and had a nice time — although he wasn't very talkative. He was attractive — kind of a cross between hottie actors Peter Horton and Eric Dane (although a bit heavier than both). After dinner, we went up to the rooftop of my apartment building and made out for a while. This was no

Colin, let me tell you! The chemistry was *definitely* there. In the online dating world, "chemistry" is a big word. Either you have it with someone or you don't, and most people expect to feel it instantaneously, which is not always a realistic expectation.

But I digress. Will wanted to see me Saturday, but my company was hosting a polo match event out in Southampton. I was allowed to bring a date, so I invited him to come along. We actually had a great time and he got along well with my co-workers. And I discovered he had a fun, mischievous side.

At the event, polo mallets were used as centerpieces on all of the tables. Will really wanted one and so did Pat, the partner of one of my gay co-workers. So as we were loading up on the bus getting ready to head back to New York City, I saw Will and Pat had each brought a polo mallet back with them and put it in the overhead compartment of the bus.

As we were about to pull out, security came on board and asked if anyone had taken a polo mallet. Will and Pat sat there completely mum. Finally, security gave up, and afterward, the two of them joked about it.

But about five minutes later, security came back on board and asked once again about the polo mallets, going down the aisle asking each row individually. They explained the mallets were part of the props for the entire month-long event and people just couldn't take them like floral centerpieces. Will and Pat sat there completely quiet, even though I kept elbowing Will to give up the mallet. Finally, with security staring us down, I pointed to the overhead compartment and they retrieved the mallets and got off the bus. It was all in good fun … I guess.

Will and I started seeing one another pretty regularly. He took me down to this hole-in-the-wall place in Chinatown that served great dim sum, and we would hang out in Central Park and have a really nice time. He wasn't much of a conversationalist — sometimes we would just hold hands at the table. But I must admit the sex was great and he was very adventurous — the kitchen counter, the bathroom, etc.

One Sunday afternoon, he asked if he could stay overnight and head to work on Monday morning from my place. I said sure, but since he didn't have clothing with him, we headed to the Gap and got him a polo shirt and khakis. (Will wasn't big on underwear.)

Then we decided to head to the market to buy something to make for dinner. I noticed his cell phone was ringing a lot during the day. He never answered it. When we got to the market, he said, "I'm just gonna go outside and check my messages. I'll meet you at the checkout in a minute, okay?"

"Sure," I said. When I finished buying the food, he was standing at the checkout talking on his phone. As soon as he saw me coming, he turned away and quickly hung up.

"My friend in New Jersey has had an emergency come up. I'm sorry, but I'm going to have to head home."

I took the food and went home and did my laundry and Sunday chores not thinking much about it. A few hours later, my phone rang.

"I did a terrible thing, Jane. Can I come over and talk to you about it?" he said.

I agreed, and he was back in about a half hour, which seemed like an awfully quick trip from New Jersey.

He proceeded to tell me the emergency wasn't his friend — but his ex-girlfriend — and when he left me, he didn't go back to New Jersey but headed downtown and spent the past two hours in a Starbucks fighting with her.

"I feel like such a shit," he said. "I can't believe I did that to you, after promising not to hurt you."

While not incredibly angry — after all the relationship was relatively new and I wasn't emotionally invested yet — I was concerned about being "rebound" girl. We talked it out for a while. He apologized profusely, and while he stayed over, it was a pretty quiet evening.

After that, I didn't hear from him. I would call and see about getting together again, and he would tell me he wasn't feeling well. Then his uncle died and he had to go to the funeral. Then it was a string of excuses until I finally pinned him down and asked what was going on. He told me he felt awful for what he had done to me — especially after promising me he wouldn't hurt me — and he didn't feel like we could continue because of it.

I noticed him online again about 18 months later and e-mailed him to see how he was doing. When I was dating him, he was working as an accountant in New Jersey and he ended up buying an apartment in Battery Park City. (It was after 9-11, so the prices were low.) He said he had taken a job as a teacher in the city.

I was curious about what had happened with him and his ex-girlfriend. He said they had gotten back together for a while, but then it crashed and burned. I was still intrigued by him, and I suppose still in my desperate mode, so I asked if he might want to get together again and he said, "No, I hurt you. I could never go back again."

I think he was being a bit melodramatic, but in hindsight, I suppose it was for the best.

Young Men With A Sense Of Humor

I should have realized after Larry, I just don't do well with younger men.

I think I am probably more serious and maybe even older than my years, but I want someone who is responsible and living in the present.

One guy contacted me and wanted to go out. He was in his late twenties and had dark brown hair and brown eyes. A bit of a Ferris Bueller. I kept telling him I wasn't interested, my usual response to younger man inquiries. He was quite the persistent bugger and would continually e-mail me. Finally, I sent him a very strong e-mail telling him I would never go out with him, and to just give up.

Well, a few days went by and I suppose it was a quiet time for dating and I was getting lonely. He was persistent, so I finally agreed to meet him for drinks. He selected a hip bar in SoHo.

He looked quite young and was rather cocky. The evening was going okay, but I didn't feel like we had much in common. And then he told me he had a present for me.

He handed me a wrapped box and when I opened it, inside was a picture frame with a printout of the e-mail I had sent him telling him I would never go out with him. He was smiling, laughing, and quite proud of himself.

"See, I told you you'd eat your words one day," he said.

I smiled politely and said it was time for us to go. He offered to get me a cab and I got in and drove away. When I got out at the corner near my apartment, I took out the picture frame and dumped it in the garbage can.

I didn't think it was *that* funny.

Guys Can Be Really Cruel

I've learned for most men, they are all about the package. You'd better be young, skinny, and gorgeous — regardless of whether they are or not!

Men are incredibly visual creatures. They want to see photos and then they will continually look at them while they are corresponding with you — and I mean continually. And they want more than just one picture — they want to see an entire collection of photos of you.

As for me, I would look at a man's photo once or twice, decide whether or not I found him attractive, and then not really check out the picture again unless it was to refresh my memory just before a first date.

But not only do men prefer lots of photos, including full body shots, they can be rather cruel and nasty, too.

I have had guys come right out and ask me what my weight is, my height, and what size clothing I wear. I have even had men ask me my bra size with absolutely no apologies. And for the most part I am truthful when I quote my weight — well, perhaps I will drop 10 lbs. But I have had them come back to me and tell me I am too old for them, too fat for them, or not pretty enough for them. And mind you, these are not just the model-type guys who are telling me this. These are the ones who live next door to you who don't have much hair on top, a really bad complexion, are 10 to 20 years older, with a beer belly. Half the time I feel like saying, "Have *you* looked in the mirror lately?"

One man and I communicated back and forth and were planning a date to meet for the first time. I found he always tried to steer the conversation to sex.

"So, Jane," he would begin. "What position do you like best?"

"Shortstop." I would joke to try and steer the conversation back to normal chatter.

"Ah … funny girl. No, seriously. How do you like to do it?"

"Do what?"

I was beginning to get the impression he was a player or at least looking for a one-night stand.

"So what are you going to wear on our first date?"

"I don't know. Haven't decided yet."

"Do you have a full-length photo of yourself?"

"No, nothing really recent."

"Hmm … what is your bra cup size?"

"Well, that's a little personal don't you think?"

"Okay, what size do you wear?"

"Does it matter?"

"Well, I'm trying to get a mental picture of you."

"I wear a size 12," I said and held my breath.

"Wow … what are you, a buck fifty?" he said. "Um, I don't think this is going to work out. Ciao!" I was still in shock, when he hung up on me.

I had corresponded with another man (late fifties, crooked teeth, balding on top) who had a very attractive personality. We really got along well on the phone and he was calling me four or five times a day in advance of the day we were to meet. One day, he finally said to me, "Jane, I feel like a kid back in high school again. I have such butterflies when I talk to you. I am so excited to meet you."

So we met for dinner one night. He seemed nice. He looked quite a bit older than 58 though. I wasn't sure if we were a match, but I was willing to give it another date to find out. The next morning, he sent me an e-mail saying, "I'm not really into the hefty Italian hips and thighs, so good luck to you!"

Why do people feel the need to be so cruel online? You can just say, "I don't think we hit it off" or "I met someone else" or whatever. There is no need to be nasty.

The world of cyber dating has definitely destroyed being socially pleasant or politically correct. I guess people feel they can hide behind their computers and will most probably never see you again, so why bother being polite?

Some Men Just Want To Sweep You Off Your Feet

I have to admit early in my online dating experience, I did meet some men who put actual thought into a date and wanted to try to sweep me off my feet.

Prince Charming, for instance. We had talked online just a bit and then he invited me to meet. He knew I was a writer, so he'd planned for us to meet at The Algonquin Hotel in New York — site of the famous Writers' Round Tables — for a drink.

When I showed up, he was wearing a suit and also brought flowers and chocolates for me. Wow! This was a nice change.

He was from an Italian background, looked like a young Tony Danza or Scott Baio, not as tall as me (which was usually a turn-off, but I was impressed with everything else, so I figured I would overlook his shortcomings), and quite charming.

We had a really nice evening and he made me feel very special. He was complimentary and we had a good time.

"Did you like meeting here?" he asked.

"Yes, this was such a great choice," I said. And I meant it.

"I figured since you were a writer, you would enjoy coming here," he said.

"I think it is really nice you put such thought into a meeting place that would appeal to me," I said.

"Well, you are a nice lady and I wanted to impress you," he said.

"That you did!" I said.

As we said our good-byes at the entrance to the hotel, he asked if he could call me again. "Definitely," I said.

He never did.

Oh well, at least for one night I felt like a princess.

The Pothead

There was a time in my online dating life when I couldn't seem to get past the third date.

Don was one of those cases. Our first date was the Feast of San Gennaro Festival in Little Italy. We walked around the festival, then had dinner in Chinatown, went out for drinks at Park Avalon restaurant (which is no longer around unfortunately) and then walked around Gramercy Park. He was intelligent, funny, and attractive — although a bit too opinionated. Ron Livingston, the actor who played Jack Berger on "Sex and the City," reminded me a lot of Don — I guess that must be why I never liked his character!

On our second date, he came over to my apartment. While he was in my living room, I walked into the kitchen to get him a beer, and when I returned, his pants were unzipped and his erect penis was showing.

"Uh ... what are you doing there?" I asked.

"Look at it, Jane. Isn't it beautiful?"

"Don! It's too early to be showing off. Why don't you just put that silly thing away for now, okay?" I said.

"Oh, sure. I just wanted you to see it."

"Very nice. Let's leave something for the imagination for awhile, okay?" I said.

While the situation was indeed bizarre, we did hit it off otherwise and there was a lot of that elusive chemistry between us. But the more conversations we had, the more I noticed he was a very angry person.

One night we were having dinner at a sushi restaurant and it took a while for the waitress to come over and take our order.

"Where the hell is this waitress?" he said so loudly people turned to stare.

"I don't know. I'm sure she'll be over in a minute," I said to try and calm him down.

"I don't know what the deal is with these fucking Asians!" he shouted. "They charge a fortune for this food and yet they take an eternity to even come and take your order. Why don't we just get the fuck out of here?"

"Don, it's 7 p.m. in New York City on a Saturday night," I said. "It's going to be busy no matter where we go. And for the rest of the night, he was surly to the waitress and extremely pissed off. That happened a lot. Whenever things didn't go according to his liking, he would lash out at whomever happened to be in his way. Thankfully, it was never me.

Something else I found a bit odd about Don was while he was a very strict vegan, he smoked pot. Here is a vegan who is very concerned about what he puts into his body, and yet he will contaminate it with pot.

On our third date, we were due to go to the movies. He came over to my apartment to pick me up and then proceeded to tell me he couldn't see me anymore. I don't recall what his exact reasoning was — perhaps something about us being too different, or he wasn't really ready for anything serious. Needless to say, I was a bit angry and frustrated I couldn't seem to get past a third date with a guy. Even a penis-showing pothead!

In hindsight, I do have to say he had a ton of courage to come and do it face-to-face. Most men didn't have the guts or courtesy to do that. Usually you got dumped via an e-mail or you had to kind of deduce you were being dumped because the guy never contacted you again. So for that I gave him credit.

But alas, that was not to be the last I heard of Don! About nine months later, I was hanging out in my apartment on a Sunday afternoon and I got an e-mail from him asking how I was doing.

"What do you want Don?" I responded in a rather cool manner. Can you tell I was still bitter because here I was nine months later *still* dating online? I sat for a few moments transfixed to the screen waiting for my mailbox to announce "You've got mail!"

And there it was.

"To be honest, Jane, I was scared. You were everything I ever wanted in a woman and it scared the hell out of me, so I ran."

I sat there staring at his email in complete shock.

"Are you serious?" I wrote back.

"Completely. And I've been sitting here ever since kicking myself. Will you at least meet me for brunch next Sunday so we can talk and I can apologize in person?"

I thought about it for a while and then decided what the heck. I didn't have much else going on and it took a lot of guts for him to admit what had happened.

We dated a few more times, but his negativity and his anger were really a drain on me. He always felt like he was being screwed and the world was against him. So I called it quits. I think he was surprised, but said he understood and apparently he had been in years of therapy working on his anger management.

From there, Don and I embarked on a friendship. Sometimes it was indeed fun, and he helped me out when I was looking to buy an apartment in the city. Since he knew a lot about architecture and had worked on his own apartment's co-op board, I used him as my sounding board for whether an apartment was built correctly. But it seemed in all cases Don saw the glass as half-empty. It was also clear he had a really serious marijuana problem — and in fact, couldn't go a day without it.

One Sunday, when we were apartment hunting, we even had to go back to his apartment in between open houses so he could take a few tokes. He had a serious problem with it and I told him he really needed to work on it. I think one time he tried to quit and lasted only 25 days. His circle of friends didn't do him any good, either. He would do a little bit of freelance work in the morning and then spend the afternoon either getting drunk or high with his friends. Frankly, how he supported himself was a mystery to me.

As I was getting ready to move out of Manhattan about three years ago, I got an e-mail from him asking how I was. We had parted on bitter terms about a year before, because he felt a friend I had set him up with to do a business deal screwed him (which was not at all the case, it was just how he always perceived everything). So I responded with one word — fine — and that was that. I guess he knew from my response not to go any further. I just had no patience for someone who was so addicted to drugs and anything I could have done would have just been enabling him.

I have always been really clear about addictive personalities and I would have nothing to do with them. Recently, a neighbor wanted to introduce me to a friend of hers who was a great guy but just happened to have a drinking problem. "No thanks," I said. Fortunately, it wasn't a lesson I had to learn the hard way.

Instant Chemistry Addicts

Speaking of addictions …

As you begin to spend more time dating online, you soon find many guys — and probably women too — who want to experience "chemistry" within the first 30 minutes of meeting you.

Perhaps there is such a thing as love at first sight, but I am more inclined to think of it as lust at first sight and not necessarily love. I can't tell you how many guys I have talked to on the phone or went out with who told me they expected to experience instant chemistry with a woman, and if they didn't, they wouldn't go out with her again.

I don't think I have *ever* fallen in love or like with someone instantaneously. Sure, I might think someone is incredibly gorgeous or quite attractive, but I really have to get to know someone in order to see if we have things in common and if we really click.

In fact, I have male friends and also my own friend's boyfriends and husbands, whom I did not find attractive in the least when I first met them, but as I grew to know them, I realized what my friends saw in them because their personality and soul were so magnificent. How can you expect to know if you are going to have a "love match" in 30 minutes?

One night I met this Russian man for drinks on the West Side. I had noticed he had been online quite a lot, so one day I contacted him and we met for a drink. He was very nice and we seemed to have a good conversation, but he seemed a bit distracted during most of the evening. As we said our goodbyes, he turned to me and said, "Jane, I think you are a nice girl, but I just didn't feel any chemistry."

I tried to investigate his statement a little further, but he admitted the way he saw it, if he didn't have an instantaneous chemical attraction (translated: an erection) within the first half hour or so, he knew the person wasn't for him. This I found quite unbelievable, but not unusual.

One of my good friends has been with a man for over 10 years. He told her a long time ago he would never marry her. He had been married once when he was much younger. It lasted for about a year, and he felt the next time he got married, it would have to be true love and he would feel like he was indeed hit by Cupid's arrow!

I can't believe people actually think like that, but they do!

I also met another man online, Mark, with whom I had a similar experience. The funny thing was he had three photos posted online and all three looked completely different. He looked like a black-haired Alec Baldwin, yet it was clear to me all the photos he had posted had been taken at different times in his life — meaning some were obviously older than others — and when I asked him which he looked most like now, he told me it was just the clothing he had on in the photos that made him look different ages. In one photo he had on a tux, so that was the "dressed-up Mark," the one where he had on a T-shirt was the "sporty Mark." Uh … okay.

We planned to meet one Saturday afternoon for an early dinner and he was going to drive in from New Jersey. He called me about 45 minutes before he was to arrive and told me he had been in a car accident and was running a little late.

"Oh my gosh," I said. "Are you all right?"

"Yeah, I'm okay," he said.

"I completely understand if you want to reschedule for another night," I said. But he blew off the accident and told me everything was fine and he would see me in about an hour-and-a-half.

When he arrived at the restaurant, he had little if any personality and was heavier and older-looking than any of his photos (kind of like Alec Baldwin looks today!). The guy who had e-mailed me and talked to me on the phone was quite lively and had a great personality. This guy was about as exciting as a bowl of oatmeal.

We sat at an outdoor table and during drinks and appetizers he spent more time looking at the dogs and people going by than at me.

"Gee, Mark" I said. "You are a lot quieter in person than on the phone. And you seem more mesmerized by the dogs passing by than my charming personality."

"I'm just not feeling it," he said. "There's no chemistry. I'm not interested."

I was temporarily startled by his disinterest and inability to even hide it. And then I put down my fork, folded up my napkin, picked up my purse, and walked away.

Goodbye and good riddance.

The Lawyer

The Lawyer contacted me one day, but he didn't have a photo posted, so I wasn't interested.

You see, when you have dated online for quite some time, you start to create some rules. One of mine was since I had my photo posted, they should, too. I don't care about all of the commentary you should get to know a person's soul first. There are just some types of individuals I know I will *never* be attracted to and just can't see myself waking up next to day in and day out.

Now, I'm not saying I'm expecting to date or marry a god. I know I'm not the perfect goddess. But there are just some basic first impressions that are important to me.

The Lawyer was relentless. I kept telling him I was not interested in corresponding with him if he didn't send me a photo. "I don't have one scanned yet," he would tell me. "Come on, take a chance!" he would say. Blah, blah, blah.

He finally talked me into meeting him for a drink and said if I didn't like what I saw, I could get up and walk out. I figured this guy was pretty sure of himself if he offered that option, and so I agreed to meet him that night.

I arrived at Merchant's, a restaurant and bar near my then apartment on the Upper East Side. It had great ambiance — comfy chairs and cozy sofas and fireplaces downstairs. It was actually quite a nice, romantic place to go — with someone who you're into.

I arrived first. When he showed up, I knew right away he wasn't my type because he seemed like a sleazy, fast-talking, ambulance-chasing type of lawyer. He was average looking, but something about him made my skin crawl. I figured I would be polite and have a drink with him. So we went downstairs, and I sat down on a chair. He chose the couch adjacent to me.

"Sit here next to me," he said.

"I'm fine right here, thanks," I said. The waitress came over to take our drink order, and he began to shamelessly flirt with her. When he wasn't flirting with other women, he was trying to impress me. I couldn't wait for the drinks to come and for the date' to be over.

As we waited for our drinks, he moved to the edge of the sofa and began to rub his hand up and down my shoulder, put his hand on my knee, and invade my personal space in general.

Now, if this was a guy I was into, by all means, knock yourself out. But with someone I had just met, I was turned off so badly my skin began to crawl.

I kept pushing his hand away and asking him to move back, but he would have none of it. So I stood up, grabbed my purse and briefcase, and started to put on my coat. He looked at me in complete shock.

"What are you doing?" he asked.

"I'm leaving," I said.

"Why?"

"Because I've asked you several times to back off," I said.

"Oh come on, you just need a drink to relax — and our drinks aren't even here yet," he said.

"Well, enjoy mine," I said and left.

My cell phone was ringing as I walked out onto the street, but I didn't answer it. If you're going to play games with me, you had best be prepared for the consequences.

It Must Be The New Haircut And Glasses

One man who looked okay in his photo contacted me, but I wasn't overly attracted to him. I probably should have stopped while I was ahead.

Since I had been single for my entire life, I had, of course, heard all of the comments I was too picky with men. I really didn't think so, but I was open to other people's opinions and since I hadn't had much success with the people whom I thought were "my type," I figured I should probably take advantage of the opportunity online to date other types of people.

"The Engineer" lived in Westchester and was very complimentary and wanted to take me out. I have to say I wasn't really attracted through our online correspondence and phone conversations, but I have known friends who have met and married men they didn't really like initially. After all this time online, I was starting to think I needed to ease up on the laundry list.

We agreed to meet on Wednesday evening for dinner in the city. Early that morning, they had forecast a major snowstorm for the afternoon and evening and I called The Engineer and asked him if he wanted to reschedule because I didn't want him driving in the bad weather.

"No, it'll be fine. I really want to meet you. Don't worry," he said.

That afternoon, the snow started to fall and became heavier and heavier. We were supposed to meet for dinner at a restaurant about a block from my house at 7 p.m. He called me at about 6:30 and said the traffic was moving really slowly and he was running late.

"Are you sure you still want to do this? It looks pretty bad outside," I said.

"Oh yes, no problem," he said. "I'll call you once I get closer," he said.

And so I sat in my apartment watching TV. An hour went by, and he finally called again.

"Second Avenue is crawling," he said. "I'm doing my best to get there."

"Okay," I said. "Be careful."

Thirty minutes later, he called again and said he finally decided to park his car in a garage uptown and would jump on a subway to get downtown because it would be much faster. I had to give him an "A" for effort at least.

The phone rang a few minutes later and he said he was about two blocks from the restaurant and I could come and meet him there. When I headed outside, the weather was completely awful, and I slipped and slid the one block to the restaurant.

When I walked in, I looked from face to face but couldn't find him anywhere. Finally, this short, stout, bald, older man with a paunch came up to me and said, "Hey, Jane! We made it."

I was stunned. Clearly the photo he had posted online was *at least* 15 or 20 years old. This man was in his late fifties.

"Oh my God, what am I going to do now?" I thought.

The maitre d' told us it would be a few minutes before our table was ready, and The Engineer excused himself to go to the bathroom. I sat there sweating it out, wondering what I was going to do, because I clearly had no interest in this person.

When he came back from the bathroom, he said, "So, what do you think? Am I what you expected?"

"Oh no!" I thought. "He can't really be asking me what I think! Is he a glutton for punishment?"

I know, I know, I've said people involved in online dating are mean and nasty, but when someone clearly misleads you with an old photo, I don't think it's fair. And here he was, asking me what I thought.

I just smiled and shrugged my shoulders. We got in the line to check our coats, and as we edged up ever closer to the coat check lady, my heart was racing. I'm wondering how I can make it through dinner and show any kind of interest in this person.

Finally, we were next in line to check our coats, and I turned to him and said, "Look, I'm sorry but I really cannot do this."

"What do you mean?" he said.

"You look absolutely *nothing* like your photo," I said.

"Oh! That's because I got a new haircut and I have new glasses," he said.

"Um, well, I don't think that's it. I'm sorry, but I just can't do this. I'm going home," I said.

And as I started to move toward the door, he said, "I just spent three hours in the car to get here and you can't even sit and have dinner with me?"

I felt like the world's biggest shit. I really did. But I hated being misled and I just didn't want to waste each other's time.

"No, sorry," I said. And I left.

I slipped and slid the entire way home and really did feel quite awful. I got into work the next day and told my co-workers what had happened. Their opinions were mixed. One felt I should have at least stayed and had dinner with him. The others agreed he deserved what he got.

Mr. Revenge

After my years of experience in online dating, I can, without doubt, strongly recommend you don't go out to dinner for a first date. If you don't get along with your date, dinner can seem interminable.

I met the man I'll call "Mr. Revenge" in Grand Central Station's market area. Based on his picture, I was on the lookout for a real cutie. He'd posted two photos and they were equally attractive. In one, he was wearing a tux (one of those pictures with the date cropped out) and the other he was on a sailboat. I walked up and down the market for quite awhile not seeing him, until I finally called his cell phone and we made a connection — he looked *nothing* like his photo and he showed up in an old plaid shirt and jeans. Not really a great way to make a first impression. I, on the other hand, had just come from work so I was in a suit and felt quite overdressed.

We had made plans to go to dinner and I was already getting a vibe this probably wasn't such a good idea. But he was insistent.

We went to one of the restaurants in Grand Central Station and I was all for just ordering an entrée and getting the heck out of there. He, on the other hand, wanted drinks, appetizers — the works.

When his appetizer arrived, he dripped some sauce on his shirt, which just happened to land on the area by his nipple. He then proceeded to take an ice cube out of his drink glass and rub the ice cube over the stain. But long after the area was quite wet and the stain was gone, he proceeded to continue to rub the ice cube over his nipple. I think he was getting off on it. Ick.

He sighed and said, "It's been nine months since I've had sex. How about you?" I had zero interest in this guy so I thought, "Why not have a little fun?" So I looked at my watch and said, "Oh, it's been about three hours now — since lunch."

I thought he was going to spit his drink out all over the table. He just looked at me and wasn't sure if I was being serious or not so I just smiled and looked away.

During dinner he proceeded to tell me a story about how he had recently been pulled over for speeding in his town.

"Can you believe this fucker pulled me over for speeding on this back road? The posted speed limit is 35 mph and I was probably going 38 or 40. What's the big fucking deal?"

"Maybe it was the end of the month and he had a quota to make," I said.

"No, he was just being a fucker. But I showed him."

"How so?"

"Well, I went back and noticed he hangs out on this old dirt road waiting for cars to speed by or blow the stop sign. So I found him one day asleep in the car and I took a photo of him napping. And I brought that to the court to show the fucker."

"You mean you didn't just pay the fine and let it go?" I said.

"Hell no! That fucker was going to pay for pulling me over! And I got him good!"

The more this guy talked, it was apparent he was extremely angry, very revengeful, and not really someone you wanted to be around very much. Not to mention his rather limited vocabulary.

When the waitress came to clear our dinner plates, she asked if we wanted dessert and I practically screamed, "No!" and then tried to soften it a bit by saying I had to get home and prepare for a presentation I had the next morning.

Mr. Revenge offered to walk me home and invited me out for an after-dinner drink. I, on the other hand, couldn't get away fast enough.

But I learned a good lesson from this date — unless you are sure you have really hit it off with someone, do *not* agree to dinner. It will be a very long night.

Unexpected One-Night Stands

Yes, there are online daters out there who are looking for one-night stands. The problem is, I didn't realize that was the situation until *after* I had slept with them.

I should qualify this by saying I found it happened much more when I was living in the city than when I moved to New Jersey. Maybe it's the faster pace of the city or the more aggressive nature of New Yorkers; I'm not really sure why.

Also, the medium of Internet dating does serve to create a buildup of sexual tension and lust.

After all, sometimes you're speaking with someone via e-mail or on the phone and you really hit it off. The more you talk to that person, the more you get attracted to them and then you can't wait to meet them. You create a relationship and bond that feels real. And after talking with someone for hours on the phone, you almost feel like you know them and have gone on a few dates with them. Also, when talking on the phone versus face-to-face, you are often less inhibited and freer to just be open and honest about yourself.

Perhaps it's not easy for someone who has never experienced online dating to understand the dynamics, but when you finally do meet the person, all you want to do is sleep with him as soon as possible. Or it might just be the fact you are lonely, horny, and just want to feel another human being hold you.

So there have been some times when I've slept with someone at the end of the first date or after a few dates because we seem really into each other. Interestingly enough, we both enjoyed ourselves immensely, but then a day or two later, I would get the inevitable phone call about how "it just moved too fast and he wasn't expecting it and he wants to take a step back and slow it down a bit."

"Okay, no problem," was my usual response, and for the most part, I meant that. Actually, there were times when I would wake up in the middle of the night to go to the bathroom, look at the relative stranger next to me and wonder what the heck I had done.

You get caught up in the excitement of it! It's a thrill that can't be matched, but afterward, you start to regret it.

And then again, sometimes you don't.

But for some reason all of these guys would just freak out. They are the ones who want to sleep with you right away, and then the next day they are having second thoughts and they don't mean taking a step back and slowing it down. They mean they never want to see you again.

Granted, I've had feelings of regret once or twice myself. But as I got over the excitement and thrill of the experience, I realized it wasn't for me.

I also learned there are certain clues to look for in a man's profile to give away he's just looking for one-night stands. As I got more experienced with online dating, I began to spot them a mile away and could act accordingly.

Although I must admit while most of my friends and I are not *"Rules"* girls (those who devoutly prescribe to the "The Rules" outlined in the book by Ellen Fein and Sherrie Schneider), it's hard to figure out when is too soon to sleep with a guy. Fein and Schneider say two months. My one friend always waits quite awhile and even makes every man she sleeps with take an AIDS test before she sleeps with him. With one particular guy, she waited six months to sleep with him, and he was still gone the next day.

So perhaps with some men it's not about the length of time, but the conquest that matters.

A Couch Interlude

I hadn't been doing online dating for too long — maybe a year or so — when I found support in the unlikeliest of places. At this point I was truly burned out with online dating — having met too many men who either weren't interested in me, didn't find me attractive, or with whom I couldn't get past the third date.

And then one day the e-mail arrived. "You are magnificent" it said, so of course, it completely caught my attention. The author didn't have a photo posted, but I really liked the tone of his e-mail. It was beautiful and spiritual and made me feel like a million bucks.

As we corresponded back and forth, my negativity about online dating was starting to show, and I spent more time talking about my bad online dating experiences than learning about him. Much to my surprise, he was patient, supportive, and I really liked having someone who listened.

Then one day, I asked him what he did for a living. He told me he was a spiritual psychotherapist. Half-jokingly, I said, "I don't know if I should date you or see you professionally." I really liked the questions he asked and how he coached me via e-mail. There was no agenda. He was just being real.

He took my remark seriously and said we could talk on the phone, and he would tell me about what he did, and we could take it from there. After awhile, I knew I had found the one — a therapist that is. A rather odd place to find one I suppose, but sometimes, when the student is ready, the teacher appears.

I had never seen a psychotherapist before and had no idea what to expect, outside of what you see on television where you lie on a couch and the therapist continually asks you what you think about whatever situation you seemed to be faced with. Clyde was completely different. He was an in-your-face therapist who called things as he saw them and really made you take a good hard look at yourself. He was also very real — using examples of his own life and struggles to make a point or show you how you weren't in this alone.

During our first session, Clyde asked me what I wanted out of my therapy and I said, "I want a relationship." Little did I know there would be so much more to uncover and deal with about myself that had absolutely nothing to do with the men I was dating. In fact, I think what made me realize I should see Clyde professionally was the fact I kept finding all of these non-committal types online — or so I thought. I was convinced these men had issues, but as the months went on, I realized every man online could not be the same. I kept running into the same situations over and over again, and you know what? It dawned on me I was the only common denominator in the equation. That was a scary thought. You never want to be the root of your own problem.

I also remember my good friend, Adele, had told me as her birthday approached that year she was giving herself the gift of psychotherapy. At first, I thought it a bit weird, but after some consideration I realized it was a darn good idea. If I wasn't happy with my life and what was happening, therapy was indeed the best gift I could give myself to help figure things out.

With Clyde's help, I realized I would be incapable of loving another human being until I learned to love and accept myself. I learned we attract our mirror in relationships so if I was attracting all of these lost, non-committal men it was because I was just as lost and non-committal. And I had so much negative energy tied to relationships and my bad experiences that Clyde asked me if deep down I really wanted a relationship when I hadn't ever experienced it as a good and positive thing. I told him adamantly I did indeed want relationship.

And you know what? It took me some four or five years to come to the realization the idea of an intimate, committed relationship truly scared the hell out of me.

In my first few sessions I realized I had some pretty serious work to do on myself. But what was most horrifying was Clyde's recommendation I take a break from dating. *What did he say? Take a break from dating!* How could I possibly do that? If I wasn't dating, how was I going to meet Mr. Right? I couldn't just sit back and not do anything. (Boy, did I have a lot to learn!)

Clyde even told me if I kept dating in the mindset I had, I was going to produce the same results — uncommitted, unavailable men. What's Dr. Phil's famous phrase? "How's it working for you?"

The reality was it wasn't working for me at all. I just kept producing more of the same.

And years later — when I finally took an eight-month break from dating — I realized it gave me the time and the space to truly focus on me and work on myself. During the time I was seeing Clyde, I never truly stopped dating. I kept my profile posted and dated here and there. But I realize, in hindsight, I let my interactions with these men completely dominate me, my everyday life, and especially my therapy. I was struggling to deal with the situation at hand with the guy-of-the-month, rather than dealing with my own issues, which I have come to realize, is the key.

I remember watching an episode of *Blow Out* where celebrity hairstylist Jonathan Antin talked to his therapist about how far he had come. Years prior, he would date anything in a skirt, but when he stopped and worked on fixing himself and becoming a better person, the woman of his dreams just showed up.

I saw Clyde for about three years in my first go-round and then took a break, during which I still dated online and had more bad luck with men. But when I finally completely took a break and started my therapy again, it was with a new perspective. This time it was all about me. And you know what? I didn't miss dating! I came to the realization the thought of having a man around 24/7 scared the crap out of me. That I was afraid to let someone get too close, because then they would see there were days when I just didn't want to take a shower.

Clyde helped me in so many ways to take my life to the next level. Did I ever expect my online dating would lead me to recreating myself and living to my fullest? Absolutely not! But I guess sometimes there are silver linings in the most unlikely of places.

9-11 Strikes Too Close To Home

I dated a man who was working in the World Trade Center on September 11, 2001.

Mike had contacted me on Match.com and we e-mailed back and forth a bit. From his profile, he fancied himself the James Bond-esque style guy. Quite the cosmopolitan man about town!

One night in the summer of 2001, we met for dinner and he brought me flowers. He had gorgeous blue eyes, dark hair, great skin, and a nice smile, and we really hit it off. We had dinner and then went for a walk in Bryant Park. We sat in the park talking for hours and then he asked if he could kiss me.

And so our relationship began. He was living in the Princeton, New Jersey area at the time (where I later moved) and was commuting into Manhattan to a new job where he was a paralegal for a big law firm at the World Trade Center. He was looking to move closer to the city, so we spent our second date apartment hunting in Brooklyn.

We found him an apartment pretty quickly, and our next few dates revolved around getting him moved in and settled. We grew close and had some great times together. As I got to know him, I realized he was anything but the cosmopolitan man about town he portrayed himself to be in his profile, and that was okay. I liked the real Mike better anyway.

We had been dating about a month when I was to leave for a long-planned vacation with a girlfriend to Club Med. It figured; when I planned the trip, I wasn't dating anyone. Now that I had someone, I was leaving town. I had no interest in meeting anyone new, so for me it was just a nice beach vacation.

It was in the heat of the summer, and Mike's new apartment had no air conditioning, so I told him he could stay at my place while I was away if he wanted. When I got back, he approached me one night and said he had accidentally knocked my bills off the dining room table and saw my rent bill — and he could never afford to pay rent on my apartment. I think it bothered him I made more money and lived a better lifestyle than he did.

What bothered me was he would never commit to dating just me. He said he just wasn't ready to commit to being serious and not dating other people yet. That really annoyed me, but I figured we'd just take it one day at a time and see what happened.

Then the morning of September 11th arrived. I was in my apartment getting ready for work, when I heard the first plane had struck the first Tower — where Mike worked. I panicked. I tried calling his apartment to see if by some odd chance he was still home, but there was no answer.

I went to the office and waited along with everyone else as the news unfolded on CNN. Where was Mike? Was he stuck on a subway? Could he be in the Tower trying to find his way down the stairs? Was he dead already? Would I ever see him again? It was one of the longest mornings of my life.

About 1 p.m., the receptionist at my office paged me and said there was someone there to see me. I raced to the reception area. She said there was a guy there who was using the phones off to the side. I was praying it was Mike. I ran right in there, and when I saw him, and gave him such a hard hug with him still sitting in the chair, I almost broke his nose. He was covered with soot but he was alive and in one piece.

He told me he was late that morning and had just emerged from the subway in time to see the second plane strike Tower number two. He followed his instincts, which said to just turn and run, but since he didn't know the area well, he ended up running around in circles. At some point, when the Towers were coming down he said he and some other commuters were running down the street and they thought we were under attack and there were bombings. They ran into a small fabric store and waited it out while the gray dust clouds roared past and then the dust settled. It wasn't until later he learned what had actually happened.

I brought him into the conference room of the company where I worked and where we had CNN on nonstop since early in the morning. They were replaying the fall of the Towers and as Mike watched, his jaw dropped and he just froze. I led him down to my office and closed the door, but he was in complete shock and unable to speak.

After awhile, he got himself together and we went home to my apartment. We had sex for hours. I don't know … perhaps it was just an affirmation we were alive and we could. He was a very intense lover. As if he was taunting God he was alive. Or he wanted to make himself feel alive. Or maybe he just wanted to forget the earlier events of the day.

The next morning, he awoke in a very sullen state which was quite understandable. He could barely speak. He had no interest in eating or drinking and was incredibly lethargic and unemotional. I'm sure he was in shock and probably dealing with post-traumatic stress syndrome and I didn't know what to do. I called Clyde and he spoke with him for a while.

We spent the next few days in a haze. The city had an eerie feeling. It's difficult to describe the mood if you weren't there experiencing it. We heard the constant sound of sirens. Every now and again a plane would fly low, and we held our breath until we realized it was probably an air force fighter patrolling the area. We tried to go donate blood, but they turned us away as they had lines and lines of volunteers.

Mike and I did a lot of talking during those days. We expressed our hurts and fears and I held him when he cried. One day we went to St. Patrick's Cathedral to pray and there were so many people inside doing the same thing. I came out and sat on the steps and just cried … and he held me.

As the weeks wore on, Mike sunk deeper and deeper into depression. His company had found temporary offices in midtown, but he wasn't going to work, and he didn't do much but sleep and sit around the house. One day, as I got up to go to work, I looked over and he made no move to get up.

"Are you going to work today?" I asked.

"No."

"Are you going to see your therapist then?" I asked, hoping for some sign of life.

"No," he said.

"Why not?"

"I just don't feel like it," he said.

I walked into the bathroom and turned on the shower. Then I walked back into the bedroom and looked at him for a while just lying on his side in bed.

"Look," I said. "I realize you have been through a bad time. A lot of people have. But you can't just sit here and do nothing. Either get up and go to work and try to get yourself back into a normal routine, go to your therapist and talk it out with her, or go back to your apartment in Brooklyn. I'm tired of you just freeloading off me and doing nothing about your situation." I felt guilty as hell for doing it, but it needed to be said.

It turned out he went to work that day ... and every day after.

A few days after 9-11, he asked if I would go back to his apartment with him to pick up some stuff. I was happy to do it, and as we rode the subway past the World Trade Center stops everyone was eerily quiet. At one point, a rescue worker got on the train and he was covered in dust and his eyes just had this hollow, dead look. The man looked like he had been through a war. He looked so exhausted. You could feel his pain.

Having Mike stay with me was the first time I had ever lived with anyone and while it took some getting used to, I really liked it. We grew closer and closer and I began to think he might as well just move in.

One evening I saw him reading *The Village Voice* looking at the apartment ads.

"What are you doing?" I asked hesitantly.

"I really need to start looking for a new place to live. I can't go back to my place in Brooklyn," he said.

I took a breath in slowly and stood there silent. I had no idea what to say.

Yet, much like other things in his life, he talked about it and talked about it, but didn't really take any action. One night I was taking a bath and I came out to find him on my computer surfing Match.com. I couldn't believe it! Here he was living in my house, eating my food, sleeping in my bed, and he was still surfing Match.com! When I confronted him, I was furious. He didn't seem to see anything wrong with it. He said he was just looking. I was incredulous! My friend said I should kick him out. But I felt bad for him — and I thought I was in love.

At another point during his stay with me, we were invited to visit a friend of mine in Connecticut for a Sunday afternoon barbecue. At the last minute, he decided not to go. When I got back to my apartment in the evening, he was cooking dinner for himself.

"Hey, how was your day?" I asked.

"Good," he said, focusing on what he was cooking in the frying pan.

"What did you do? Just hang out here?" I asked.

"Actually no, I met Laura for lunch." Laura was his ex-girlfriend.

"Oh," I said. That was about as much as I could muster. I was so taken off-guard. But I wasn't going to let this go.

"Was this planned for a while?" I asked.

"She had called the other day, but I wasn't sure if I was up to it," he said.

"So what did you guys talk about?" I asked. I was trying to sound nonchalant, but inside, I couldn't believe this was happening.

"She told me she still has feelings for me."

"And ..."

"And I went to see if I felt the same way," he said.

"Do you?" I asked, holding my breath.

"I don't know."

Once again, I was furious. Here I was, taking care of him and he was treating me like crap. But as usual, I took it. I liked this guy, I didn't want to let him go, and we had been through so much together.

One Saturday not too long after, he asked if I would go apartment hunting with him in Queens, so I reluctantly agreed. We took a subway to Forest Hills, and in the middle of our ride, the train came to an abrupt halt. We sat there for about 20 minutes. "He has a gun!" we heard, and everyone was looking at the subway car behind us. Everyone began screaming and freaking out.

"He's headed this way!" someone shouted. We all ran for the opposite car in a frenzy, but the door was locked. Mike pushed me down under the seat and threw himself on top of me. Then, amid the chaos, we realized if we couldn't get into the next car because the door was locked, the gunman wouldn't be able to get into our car either.

We sat back up on the chairs. I was shaken and frozen. Mike was incredible and comforted me and held my hand. I was very impressed he tried to protect me when usually he acted like a wounded deer. These traumatic experiences made me feel closer and closer to him.

A couple of weeks later, my phone rang.

"Hi!" Mike said, sounding very upbeat and excited.

"Hi yourself."

"Guess what? I have great news! I found an apartment in Queens," he said.

My heart sank. I guess deep down I didn't think he was going to move out and I thought we would stay together.

"Oh? Really. Wow. I guess I kind of thought you would be staying here with me."

"I know, but right now I just need some time alone to get myself together. And this is really a great place and I can move in next week," he said.

Needless to say, I was not happy and all of my old feelings of abandonment reared their ugly heads once again.

So in a replay of one of our earlier activities, we got Mike moved and settled, but I noticed he was distant. After he moved nearly all of his things out of my apartment, he stopped calling me or returning my calls. After awhile, I couldn't take it anymore and finally put him on the spot.

"Mike, what's going on? I *never* hear from you anymore and I feel like I'm always chasing you down," I said.

"Look, I told you I just need some space to think things out."

"Yes, you've told me," I said. "But I feel like I am getting punished here and all I've ever done for you is help you out."

"Actually, that's part of the problem," he admitted. "You've seen me cry and you've seen parts of me I don't normally show to anyone else. I'm embarrassed by how I behaved in those days after the attacks and I just don't think I can be with you anymore because of that."

"Are you serious?" I said. "I found those times really important because we were being our most vulnerable and sharing our true feelings with one another. There is nothing to be embarrassed about."

"Maybe for you, but not for me," he said. And then, he slowly faded out of my life.

A few weeks later he called me, and was very upbeat, and asked me to meet him for lunch that day. He sounded happy and I was hoping it was good news for me. When I arrived at the diner, I noticed he was carrying the overnight bag with my makeup and stuff I had left at his apartment. "This is not a good sign," I thought.

We sat down and he seemed very excited. "I have great news," he said. "I think I met 'the one.'"

I sat there, incredulous. Evidently, "the one" was a girl he met commuting on the subway. He went on and on about how great she was and how he really liked her and I just sat there in disbelief. I could feel the emotion building inside me, and when I could finally hold it in no longer, I burst into tears. I quickly gathered my things and said, "I cannot believe you invited me here to lunch to tell me you've met 'the one' when you know how much I care about you and what I have done for you these past few months!" I put on my coat and left. What was he thinking? I mean, this was the middle of a workday! I headed back to the office with tears streaming down my face. (Good thing at least I had my makeup bag with me. I was about to need it!) When I got back to my office, I sequestered myself behind closed doors.

A few hours later, I got an e-mail from him telling me he was so sorry he hurt me and he could see how much pain I was in. We talked a few times on the phone after that, and I cried and begged him to come back. He would have none of it. He was clearly over me. He used me for what he needed.

A few months later, I had started dating someone else, and Mike called. I was quite happy inside when I learned the girl he thought was "the one" had dumped him. I remember him calling me and talking to me about it. It was rather a weird situation.

Here he was practically crying to me over a woman who dumped him when he had in turn done the same to me ... and yet inside, I was taking particular pleasure in the scenario.

We rekindled our friendship and I invited him to my 40th birthday bash. It turned out the man I was dating, The Perfect Guy, (who you'll soon learn about), stood me up. Mike offered to help me get all the gifts back to my apartment, and one thing led to another and you guessed it, we ended up sleeping together. It felt great — like old times — and I wondered if we would get back together. When I asked him what he was thinking, he was, of course, non-committal. He wanted to see if he still had feelings for me, but after all this time, still wasn't ready to commit to dating just me.

We saw each other again once or twice, but he said he wanted to play the field. He kept saying he didn't think we were right for each other, but I suspected he still had issues with my having seen him crying and "weak."

About two years later, I re-launched my business after taking a brief hiatus to join the corporate world, and I needed a copywriter to help out. I knew he was a good writer, and was of course, yet again, out of a job. So I hired him to work for me on a freelance basis. From a business standpoint, it was working out great — but it was a little awkward personally. I still had feelings for him, and it was hard to see him on a daily basis — especially when I knew he was still surfing Match.com. He would come in and tell me about his dates or have his girlfriends call him at the office.

And then the blackout hit in August that year. I had been out of town in the Berkshires to see a client and was heading back into the office that morning. Mike had told me the day before he was feeling quite ill with stomach pains and if he didn't feel better, he might need to go the doctor. When the blackout hit, I was stuck on a Metro North train for hours. When I finally got to a friend's house, I called Mike's but there was no answer. And then I called a friend with whom we shared the office loft space, and she said he hadn't been feeling well, and when the blackout hit he just walked down the stairs and left.

I called his house for the next few days but there was no answer. I began to get worried. I called his parents and they hadn't heard from him. I contacted some of his friends and they hadn't heard anything either. When he didn't show up for work the next week, my worry turned to panic. I called the NYPD to place a missing person's report, but they wouldn't let me do it because I wasn't family — and his family didn't seem too worried about the fact no one had heard from him.

So the next day, a friend of mine who worked for the NYPD got some local cops in Queens to go to his apartment. They rang the doorbell, but there was no answer. The neighbors hadn't seen him in days. The police were outside his apartment door and thought they smelled gas, and it was sufficient cause to get them to try and break the door down to gain entrance. As they worked on the lock, I started to get weak in the knees — thinking we were going to find him lying dead on the floor.

There was no sign of him in the apartment, but all of his things were there. I headed back into the city on the subway completely baffled.

The next morning I came in to my office to a voice mail from Mike: "Stop calling me. Stop calling my friends and family. I am fine, but I am *never* coming back to work." I have no idea what happened or why he chose not to come back. I wondered if the blackout gave him flashbacks to 9-11.

Since then I've seen his profile on Match.com. He's apparently moved back to New Jersey where he grew up. And his profile still portrays this James Bond-esque mystery man he always wished he could be. It wasn't the real Mike I knew and fell in love with. But apparently he didn't like that guy.

Dangerous Liaisons

I can't believe how incredibly careless I was regarding my safety. I got so caught up in the romance of the experience I did the kinds of things you read about in newspapers — imprudent, naïve things that potentially put my life at risk.

There was one incident where I had been e-mailing and IM-ing with this guy for a few weeks. We were trying to plan a date to get together. I worked Monday through Friday and he worked at a car dealership on weekends, so getting our schedules together was challenging. He also had an interesting back-story in that he used to be a professional billiards player and was in a plane crash at LaGuardia Airport where he literally just walked away. Seemed like a lucky guy.

One Saturday afternoon, I was sitting in my PJs in the comfort of my apartment IM-ing with him, and out of nowhere, he asked me to take a train out to Long Island and meet him. I typed back I couldn't possibly do that. But actually, it sounded enticing. I got caught up in the romance and mystery of it all. He told me he would rent a room at the Huntington Hilton and we would have a nice romantic night.

I guess I must have been especially lonely and horny that day, because I showered and got dressed and headed out on the Long Island Rail Road. He picked me up at the train station and drove me to the hotel. He looked exactly like his photo, but seemed a bit distant. He had already checked into the room, and when I walked in, there were candles lit and romantic music playing. When I went into the bathroom, there was shampoo, and a puff sponge, and tons of nice lotions and amenities laid out on the counter.

"Did you get all of this for me?" I asked.

"No, that's my stuff," he said, which I thought was a bit weird (a true metrosexual I guess).

We ordered food from room service and I have to say I wasn't really feeling the chemistry, but as so often happens, we end up in bed anyway. But I noticed throughout sex he kept his eyes closed, which is a bit strange to say the least.

The next morning, I awoke to one miserable and cranky guy. "I have a horrible migraine," he said. So he slept for a while and then said he needed to get to work. We got dressed and he dropped me off at the train station on Sunday morning without even offering to stop for coffee.

Later that night I got an e-mail from him. "I couldn't believe how fat your are," he wrote. "You're an ugly slob. I had to keep my eyes closed the entire time we were having sex just to be able to get through it." I was shocked and mortified.

Had I not been a willing participant, I could have been raped. Thank goodness God was watching over me and nothing violent happened.

Let me tell you, I was out for revenge. I took it upon myself to conduct an e-mail campaign to all of the girls on the online dating site who lived in his area. I told them I had gone out with him and how nasty he was to me and recommended to not answer any e-mails from him. It was girl power to the nth degree because I had so many women write me back and tell me what a horrible experience that must have been for me, they had been corresponding with him, and would immediately cut it off.

Close to a year later, I got an e-mail from him. He apologized for his behavior and said he felt really bad. Maybe he did indeed have a soul or perhaps he was tired of not getting any responses from all of the other women online whom I had told my story to!

Dangerous Liaisons Part Two

Another incredible exercise in stupidity was with Paul, an ambulance-chasing lawyer from Connecticut who bragged about his television ads during our first conversation and hinted he was Connecticut's version of New York's infamous Jacoby & Meyers law firm.

We had been e-mailing and talking on the phone for quite some time. We had these incredible, lengthy conversations. Not the usual banter. These conversations really made me think. He would ask me profound questions or we would have these philosophical discussions and I swear by the time I got off of the phone with him my brain literally hurt. But at the same time, I found it rather exciting.

He was also challenging me a lot as far as getting out of my comfort zone ... he told me he used to date a lot of strippers and he still had some for friends. He rode a Harley and had some friends who were on drugs and he said he'd tried some himself when he was younger. Me, I hadn't even tried pot. He seemed like a straight-laced lawyer who definitely had an edgy side. I think with all this talk about his wild side, he was testing me to see if I could handle it.

One beautiful fall Saturday, he invited me to go to Connecticut where he lived. He picked me up at the train station and, I was shocked, because of course, his photo — which made him look like a cross between Alex Trebek and Tom Selleck — was about 15 years younger and 50 lbs. lighter than the man who greeted me at the train station. No matter how many times it happens, the "old photo" trick always seemed to take me by surprise.

But he was very nice and he drove me to his gorgeous house and gave me a tour. It was such a nice day, and he invited me for a ride out on his Harley. I had never been on a motorcycle. The changing leaves along the country roads were magnificent. The only problem was he used helmets without face guards, so as we drove at high speeds, I felt like I was being given an instantaneous face-lift from the pressure of the wind. And my eyes were tearing continuously even though I had sunglasses on.

After the ride, we stopped at some beautiful inns to take a look around. (Yet for lunch, he took me to a crappy coffee shop in another town. Go figure.) We then went to play pool at some real biker hangout — once again, I think he wanted to see how I would react. (For the record, I beat the pants off him.) Later we went back to his house, ordered Chinese food and talked for hours.

At around 1 a.m. — I didn't even realize what time it was — he announced I was a really nice girl, but he didn't feel any chemistry and he was going to take me to the train to head home. "It's a little late for me to be taking a train back to the city, don't you think?" I said.

"I guess you're right," he said. "Why don't you stay in my daughter's room, and take the train in the morning? She's away on a trip."

Lucky for me, he was a perfect gentleman and nothing happened. No one knew where I was, and he could have drugged my drinks and raped me, or even worse. Someone was undoubtedly watching out for me and to this day I am quite thankful for my luck.

The New York State Trooper

Chuck was a retired New York State Trooper.

He had contacted me online and we had chatted a bit. He lived in upstate New York and as it turned out, one weekend I was heading past his town to go up to the Berkshires to meet a friend of mine. We were going to a workshop at Kripalu, a spiritual wellness center.

When I mentioned what my plans were, he said, "Why don't you get off at my exit? We'll meet for a quick hello at the rest area and we can see what we think."

It made sense, as I was going that way anyway.

It turned out Chuck had been divorced for a few years and had a young daughter who lived with him half the time. He was 45, already retired, of Dutch descent, and seemed to have a lot of time on his hands, which was a welcome change. I was growing tired of dating the executives who were so successful they worked night and day and had no time for me.

I met Chuck at the rest area. His straight brown hair and piercing blue eyes matched his photo perfectly. He seemed a little shy, which I found endearing. He had taken the time to MapQuest directions for me to get to my friend's house in The Berkshires and he brought me a bottle of water and a snack for the rest of the trip.

We made plans to meet on my way back and to spend the day together.

During my time away, he called and left messages and we chatted a bit. He seemed nice and fun and had a good sense of humor.

When I called him the morning of our proposed meet-up, he told me his ex-wife had flaked and he had his daughter that day. He suggested I stop over and pretend I was just a friend and we could go out to lunch with his daughter. I wasn't overly thrilled, but I agreed.

And so I met his daughter and saw his house — which had an incredibly large collection of Hot Wheels cars mounted in a glass box on the wall. Boys will be boys, I guess.

He took me to a Dutch bakery a few towns away which provided us with a nice scenic drive. I was really enjoying our time together.

"Why don't you come back next weekend when my ex-wife will have my daughter?" he said. I agreed.

The next weekend, he picked me up from the train station, and when we arrived at his house, it was clear he was in the process of fixing up his house. He was in the middle of laying floor tile in the kitchen, evidently more convenient to tackle while his daughter was away.

He was running behind in completing the project and asked if I wouldn't mind helping him finish the job so we could have more time free to spend together the rest of the day. I really didn't mind, and afterward, we spent the day driving around sightseeing and having a nice time. His cell phone kept ringing and he looked at the number, saw it was his ex-mother-in-law, and said he wasn't going to answer it. When we got home, there were also quite a number of messages on his home answering machine and when he finally listened to them, it turned out his ex-wife had been taken to the hospital with a medical emergency and he had to go pick up his daughter.

"I'm sorry, Jane. I hate to do this, but I'm going to have to take you to the train," he said. I was a little taken aback by the entire thing, but I agreed and dutifully went home.

We talked a few more times on the phone, but there always seemed to be some crisis or another involving his daughter and his ex-wife and I realized he just wasn't available. I learned a lot from this experience: first off, to become really clear that while I totally respected a man who put his children first — the way it should be — I didn't want a man who already had children. I deserved to be first in a man's life.

The "Perfect" Guy

If there ever was a date who looked good on paper — no, make that look GREAT on paper — Roger was it.

A graduate of Princeton University, Roger came from a wealthy family from New Orleans and had been an Olympic swimmer. When I met him, he was working as a CEO at a biotech company. He was articulate, funny, and very good looking. On paper, he really was the perfect guy, and to this day no one seems to compare to him in that regard.

Roger and I met on eHarmony — a dating site that guides you through a personality test and then matches you up based on their criteria for good chemistry. With other sites, you can sift through photos and profiles and pick your own match. Roger and I made it through all of the prepared questions they had potential matches go through and chatted for hours on line and IM-ed. When I finally agreed to meet him, I had never seen a photo, but I was so taken with him it didn't matter. Much to my pleasure he was *gorgeous* — kind of like Patrick Dempsey. But he had no clue he was.

Unfortunately, Mr. Perfect had his issues. Roger had been married and divorced twice — both times to his "grandmother" as he put it — very strong-willed, difficult women. He was very wary about getting married again and making a third mistake. His first wife was a lawyer who ended up cheating on him soon after they were married. His second wife suddenly decided she didn't want to have children — and was so terrified of getting pregnant she even refused to have sex with him.

Roger was a workaholic, and therein laid the problem. He was trying to build his biotech firm and he worked every hour of the night and day, even weekends. It was very difficult to get time to see him and I often found myself begging him to plan dates with me weeks in advance.

And while he could carry on a conversation about practically anything, when it came time to express his feelings about me, Roger was utterly speechless. One night we were lying in bed and I kept pushing to find an answer to how he was feeling about me or where he thought this was going.

And after some stuttering and sighs, he said to me, "Ask me how much I made this year."

So I said, "I don't know, how much?"

And he said, "Fifteen hundred dollars."

He proceeded to tell me as CEO of a start-up biotech firm he didn't get a salary and was just in it for the stock options. Since he didn't really make any salary and didn't know when he would make money — or if this job would even work out — he couldn't possibly get into a serious committed relationship.

I found this to be a pretty common thread in a lot of my relationships. If a man's career wasn't going the way he thought it should, then he couldn't involve himself in a relationship. I don't know why one had to preclude the other and often felt with the love and support of a partner, oftentimes things with a bad job or whatever might turn around, but they never seemed to see it that way.

So while I had this "great" guy on paper, I wasn't really happy in the relationship and I suppose I really didn't "have" him anyway. The Perfect Guy was quite the elusive fellow. We didn't really see each other very much, and when we did, he was somewhat distant, and he wasn't very romantic. Sex with him was very mechanical — he was always in his head thinking about doing this move or that move right instead of just losing himself in the moment.

For some reason I found it very important to hold on to The Perfect Guy, but it was actually one of the most unsatisfying relationships I had ever had. We spent more time IM-ing with one another or on the phone than actually being together physically. Maybe he found that to be enough, but I certainly didn't. In addition, he would never let me visit him in New Jersey. I wondered if perhaps he was married, but I had all his numbers, so it didn't seem likely. I think he just lived in a terribly messy apartment or one that wasn't really decorated and he was afraid to show his true self. The reason I suspected this is because one time, unexpectedly, he had to give me a ride in his car and it was a filthy dirty mess.

But the last straw was on my 40th birthday.

I was throwing myself a great party at a friend's New York hotel. Roger was to be my date. A few hours before the party, he called me from his cell phone and I could tell he was in his car on the road.

"Are you on the way into the city?" I asked.

"Actually I'm on my way to Philly for a business meeting," he responded.

At 4 p.m. on a Sunday afternoon, he chose to attend a business meeting in Philadelphia and stand me up for my 40th birthday party! That was it. Perfect or not, he made it too hard to build a relationship.

But for some reason, I just couldn't let go of the fact he really was the perfect guy on paper. I held out hope if his company took off, it would click for us. Every now and again I would contact him to see how he was doing. For awhile, he was very busy and not into dating. Then he said maybe we should work together first, as he was very gun-shy about relationships and really needed to see if he could trust me as a co-worker and friend before getting involved in a relationship. I suppose I was desperate and so I agreed.

The plan involved two of his friends who had an advertising agency and wanted to go after the advertising account for the British Virgin Islands. Since my specialty was in travel public relations, he thought we would all be a good fit and we began to work on a proposal with us all consulting together. And then I had a potential client who needed some advertising work done and I invited Roger and his friends to meet with the client to try and give them some business as well.

It turned out to be a disastrous situation, and he and his business associates behaved badly toward me. We all had to travel to Atlanta one day for a meeting with my client and they acted like frat boys. Once they had cleared the security line at the airport they just went ahead on their own without waiting for me. They got themselves breakfast and headed to the gate without asking if I wanted anything, and on the way home they had three seats together leaving me to sit alone. I suspected they were plotting something with my client behind my back which made me very uncomfortable.

But months later, of course, I was still thinking about Roger. Out of sheer desperation, loneliness, and the fact I still believed he had the potential to be an actual "Perfect Guy," I called him. I was also in a major dating famine. This time, he told me all he could offer was friendship because he was now in a very serious relationship. Sure. Of course. I said "no thanks" and went on my way.

I don't know why I kept going back to him. I honestly think it was his résumé. After all, who wouldn't want to say they were married to a Princeton grad, Olympic swimmer, and CEO? In reality, I spent more time *wanting* to be with him than actually *being* with him.

Now I know what people mean when they say you can be in a relationship and yet feel terribly alone.

The Ferryboat Captain

One thing I can say about my online dating life is it was never boring!

Where else would I meet men from so many different walks of life, like Vinnie, the ferryboat captain. Yes, a ferryboat captain!

Vinnie — who was about 5' 7", burly, and with rugged features — owned a boat docked at Pier 29 in downtown Manhattan. It was an honest to goodness ferryboat dating back some 100 years.

For our first date, we met at a bar downtown and then walked over to see his boat because I was so intrigued by it. The boat was permanently docked at the pier and he often rented it out for private parties.

But Vinnie was also an antique collector — maritime pieces mostly — and the ferry was jammed with dusty old maritime stuff. In fact, you could barely walk around in some parts of it because of all the old dusty crap shoved in there.

I must admit sitting out on the deck overlooking the Hudson River on a breezy summer evening was very romantic and a rare and unique opportunity!

On our second date, Vinnie invited me over to the boat where he cooked me dinner — pasta with shrimp. It was a delicious meal, and once again we sat out on the deck overlooking the river. This was definitely an experience other New Yorkers could only imagine. (Unless, I suppose, they had a party on his boat.)

As our relationship progressed, I spent a few nights with him on the boat, although it did feel a bit like living in a college dorm as he had people who worked for him living on the boat as well. Had some money been invested into renovating the vessel, it would have been an amazing place to live and have parties; however, for whatever reason he chose not to invest in it or didn't think it needed to be renovated. As a matter of fact, one time when he was at my apartment — which I likened to a Pottery Barn catalogue — he commented we clearly had totally different decorating styles. And I could tell from the tone of his voice he didn't much like mine!

One day Vinnie invited me to visit him at New York's big antique show on the Piers where he was trying to sell some of his maritime collection. It was nice to see a different side of him, although I did find him a bit aloof.

On the nights he came over to my house for dinner, he often showed up dirty after what must have been a day of working on the boat. His fingernails were filthy and he smelled like a grease monkey. Evidently he thought it too much bother to take a shower before he came over.

One evening, he told me he'd gone out fishing and caught some fresh fish he was going to bring over and cook for me. I waited and waited for him to arrive. He showed up about two hours late, and as he got off the elevator, he announced he had forgotten the fish at home! Oh well ... so much for the fish. We ordered in Chinese instead.

That night as we were watching television, he fell asleep on the couch and when it got late, I turned off the TV and invited him to come into the bedroom.

"In a minute," he said. He spent the entire night out on the couch snoring away.

Vinnie was also not the most well-mannered guy. For instance, he thought nothing of farting in bed right in front of me.

A few weeks into our "relationship," he informed me someone made an unsolicited offer to buy the boat from him. He had no plans to sell and didn't even have the boat up for sale, but it was an interesting offer. The big dilemma, for him, was where would he live if he sold it?

Within two weeks, he had accepted the offer and announced he planned to go live in the Catskills for a while until he figured out his next move.

"Will you come to New York and will I see you again?" I asked. (Boy, was I getting to be a broken record or what with this desperation?)

"I don't know, Jane," he said. "It's not like I planned this, but I do need to figure out my life."

And that was my tale on the high seas — or at least the Hudson River.

Venturing Beyond My Comfort Zone

I must admit I am pretty much a white bread kind of girl when it comes to men.

I didn't date very many Jewish men online nor did I date anyone of color, until I met Nate, a younger, aggressive Korean lawyer. Nate was a transplant to New York from Washington, D.C. and he was the CEO of a high-tech startup (starting to sound familiar?).

We met for drinks and dinner at a hip restaurant and he was charming, driven, and interesting — although he wouldn't get off his cell phone for the first hour of the evening.

I finally asked if I could see his cell phone, and when he gave it to me, I shut it off and dropped it in my purse. "You can have it back at the end of the night," I said. He was surprised, but didn't argue.

A few dates later, we went back to his place and things got hot and heavy. We were down to our underwear and he was very much into rubbing himself against me — but that is as far as I let him go. The funny part was that the next day he called me and said he was all chafed and his penis was killing him. I actually thought it was pretty funny, but he was very seriously concerned about how much it hurt — so much so he actually said he needed to become celibate for a while so he could heal.

So we didn't date for a week or so, and then he called and we went out again and this time, we slept together. The next morning — a Sunday I think — he woke me up and rushed me out of the bed and into the shower, telling me he had an appointment with a real estate agent to see a new apartment and I had to leave pronto.

I didn't like getting the bum's rush. A few days later, he proceeded to tell me how he really needed to focus on his career and to make something of himself. In part I felt bad for him because he was a first generation Korean in America and he seemed to have a lot of family pressure to achieve and be a success.

I am sure it was just a story. Either he wasn't interested in me or wasn't interested in dating, but in any event, we never saw each other again.

Trying To Get Over Myself

I suppose I'm a snob when it comes to dating. No, I'll admit it. I *am* a snob when it comes to dating.

I know, I know — it might not seem like it. I dated the farty ferryboat captain and a bi-polar Ronald McDonald, but those were against my better judgment and in moments of desperation. *Really.* Deep down I really see myself with a successful man who makes a good living, drives a good car, has a good education, and lives in a nice neighborhood.

Perhaps it is the old Cinderella curse from my upbringing — as young girls we are told the "Prince" will come to whisk us away and we will live happily ever after. I wasn't like a lot of my friends who expected the man I married to support me 100% and make an excellent living, but I did want this person to have a job or career I would be proud of talking about to my friends.

One day, not long after I found out my "Perfect Guy" Roger was now in a serious relationship with someone, I realized I couldn't pine for him any longer and I really needed to move on. At about the same time, I got an e-mail from Justin. Hey, I had a live one here! He was 36 years old and lived in Staten Island. Borough. I didn't really do borough. If you're not a New Yorker, "borough" means the other parts of New York City besides the island of Manhattan, including Brooklyn, Queens, The Bronx, Staten Island, etc. (And Mike doesn't count.)

But Justin wrote me very nice notes about how attractive I was. His profile didn't list his career, so I asked what he did and he told me he worked for the City of New York.

"What do you do for the City of New York?" I asked. I mean, that could be anything from repairing streets to the Deputy Mayor.

"I work for the Department of Sanitation," he replied.

"Uh oh," I thought. This was a little disconcerting.

"What do you do for the Department of Sanitation?" I asked.

"I pick up garbage," he replied.

Oh no! Could there be a worse job one could have than a garbage man? Actually, when I told a close friend she said it would be worse if he was a porn star. Yes, I suppose that would have been worse. But not by much.

I have to say his admission stopped me in my tracks for a moment. Could I really bring myself to date a garbage man? Here I was a college educated, successful woman with my own business and I was about to date a garbage man? I couldn't have landed any farther from my "Perfect Guy" if I tried.

And then a friend said it really shouldn't matter what he did, but who he was as a person. So I decided to get over myself and meet him for coffee on a Sunday afternoon. I suppose it helped he did indeed have a four-year college degree and had majored in psychology. He was also studying to get his private pilot's license. He wasn't stupid. I'm not exactly sure why he chose to be a garbage man. Does anyone really choose it as a profession? Does anyone say, "Mom, when I grow up, I want to be a garbage man!"

I invited Justin to meet me at a cool coffee house on the Upper West Side. I arrived first, and the coffee house was overflowing with people. So I sat on a bench out front waiting for him. He was late. After about 15 minutes, I saw him crossing the street wearing some sort of strange hat, and I thought, "Oh boy … here we go."

I was being terribly judgmental right from the beginning and found myself looking for something that would make this not work out. When he got closer, I got a better look at him. He had a beautiful complexion, chiseled features, and nice blue eyes.

It was clear we were never going to get a seat in the coffee house, so we decided to walk down the street and see what we can find. We came across an Italian restaurant, and since neither of us had eaten, we decided to grab a bite.

I noticed Justin didn't put his napkin on his lap, and when our salad was served, he seemed a little embarrassed.

"I was never good with all this silverware on the table and trying to figure out which is the right fork to use," he said, and laughed nervously.

"I know. It can be intimidating. Let me share a little trick with you I learned years ago. You just work your way from the outside to the inside," I said. And off we went. But the fact he admitted he didn't know what to do was heartwarming to me.

He seemed very nervous, and I felt bad for him. But we had a nice conversation, and after lunch he asked if I wanted to take a walk in Central Park with him, which was just a few blocks away. It had started raining, and I had an umbrella and he didn't. As we crossed the street, I slipped (must have been the oil and rain mixed together on the pavement) and went face down in the street like a ton of bricks. Could I have been *more* embarrassed?

Justin quickly reached down and helped me up. To lighten up the moment I said, "See, I'm already falling for you!"

"I'd better hold your hand to make sure you don't fall again," he said. I liked that. My knee was killing me … and I could feel the blood dripping down my leg. But at least I didn't tear a hole in my pants!

We walked around the park and talked for a long time. Conversation came very easily between us, and I had to admit Justin was a really nice, gentle, kind man. After awhile, he leaned over and kissed me, and the chemistry was definitely there.

It started to rain harder, so we left the park and walked along the Upper West Side. He was definitely into hanging out longer, but I was getting tired, my knee was swelling, and I was ready to go home.

"Did you want to go grab a cup of coffee and get out of the rain?" he said.

"Um, that would be nice, but my knee is really starting to hurt and I have some things to take care of before Monday morning," I said.

I think part of my desire to escape the date was I simply didn't want to be falling for a garbage man. This couldn't be happening, could it?

"Oh come on, Jane. I am having a really great afternoon. Let's spend some more time together."

"Yeah, it's nice, isn't it, but I'm sorry. I really have some things I have to take care of," I lied and made a hasty retreat. We kissed goodbye at the entrance to the subway and off he went bounding down the stairs. I hailed a cab, sank into the back seat, and let out a deep sigh. What the heck was I getting myself into?

A few days later, Justin called and invited me over to his house for dinner. He wanted to cook for me, he said. So I took the ferry over to Staten Island and he picked me up and brought me back to his apartment.

It wasn't the fanciest apartment and was by no means in an elegant doorman building, but it was nice and he had decorated it quite attractively and much better than I would have expected from a guy. They say you can tell a lot about a man from how he decorates his home and this said Justin wanted to live in a nice home that was warmly decorated. He even had a cloth tablecloth and cloth napkins. (I didn't even do cloth when people came for dinner!)

He served a lovely salad, with shrimp, bread, and we had some wine. It was a delicious dinner, and I appreciated the effort, as I couldn't remember a time when a man had actually cooked me dinner in his apartment.

Afterward, we hung out on his couch and talked for a long time.

"This is nice, Jane," he said. "I'm having a really good time with you."

"Yeah, I am too ..."

"I sense a 'but' there," he said.

"Well, to be completely honest, I'm still having major issues with what you do for a living, and I'm not sure I can get past it."

"I understand that. I'm glad you tell me what you are really thinking and I hope you always feel that way."

"Yeah, but where do you see this really going?" I mused.

"To be honest, Jane, I see this going all the way."

I was surprised, yet had this very weird feeling like there was a different vibe here than I have ever had with a man. And I have to admit, for the first time in my life, I felt very comfortable with Justin. I felt safe, like I could tell him anything and there was something special about him.

"Maybe I should take a closer look at this man and get over myself," I thought.

And so we began our relationship.

The situation was made a little more difficult, however, by the fact I was in the process of moving from Manhattan to New Jersey. In just about two weeks after we met, we were now living over an hour apart.

Whenever a friend would ask how my dating life was going, I would mention I met someone. Inevitably, the second question out of her mouth would be, "So, what does he do for a living?" A person's career is such an important status symbol in our society, and I am the first to admit I feel the same way. I always want to know what someone does, because I guess it feels like their career somehow defines who they are — smart, successful, lazy, whatever.

As for Justin, his parents were both immigrants from Newfoundland. His father died when he was nine years old and he never really had anyone to guide him. His mother checked out at that point and the four kids were sort of on their own. Justin had dropped out of high school, but ended up getting his GED and went on to get a college degree which I found admirable. I just didn't understand why he never did anything with it.

He told me after he graduated, he was a bit lost and didn't know what to do with himself. A friend told him he was taking the test to become a sanitation worker so Justin figured what the heck, and took it as well. When he was called up for service, I don't think he really planned on making a career out of it. But he also said on Staten Island, a lot of the immigrants there feel it is a safe way of life — they have a guaranteed job for 20 years and then they get a pension for life. They're "set."

Justin was about six years into his career as a sanitation worker, and I could tell he didn't really like it. (Seriously, who could *like* it?) But I think he felt he was on his way and couldn't really walk away now. I was from a totally different mentality — find a job you like, leave the Sanitation Department, and chalk it up to a job you worked at for six years. He viewed it as a "life sentence" where he at least had to put in 10 or 15 years to feel like he walked away with something.

I knew I made more money than Justin. So I felt bad whenever we went out, and more often than not, I offered to split the check. My friends and family were so mad at me over this one. "The man is supposed to *always* pay," they would tell me. Maybe they were from a different generation or maybe I felt like I wasn't worthy enough to have a man pay for me all the time. Maybe it was a little of both.

Like most relationships, there were good things and bad things. I loved the fact Justin would get up on Sunday mornings and make me breakfast. I liked that he would look at me and just stare and say he wanted to take in my beauty and enjoy how I looked. He was great with my puppy, Sophie. If only he wasn't a garbage man! And he drove a really old, crappy car, which I found embarrassing.

When it came time for Christmas, Justin completely surprised me. We had gone shopping a lot together for various things, and one time I picked up a purse just in passing and put it down again.

When I opened my Christmas gifts, Justin had bought me that purse. I couldn't believe he even noticed or remembered it, but he did. He also bought me a gorgeous leather jacket in my favorite color — lavender. The garbage man did good. Really good.

I kept asking Justin what we were going to do for New Year's Eve. He kept avoiding the question, and then about three nights before New Year's, I finally had my answer. "You want a serious relationship, and that's not what I want," he said during a phone call. "I think we should stop seeing each other."

"Are you kidding? You are breaking up with me now? What happened to 'seeing this go all the way?'" I began to cry.

"Jane, don't cry. I don't know what to say, but I don't want you to cry," he said.

"Well, what should I say when you tell me you are breaking up with me?" I said.

"Let's just think about this. I will call you tomorrow, okay?"

As I sat and thought this over, I don't know what was more upsetting: the fact I was getting broken up with, or a garbage man was breaking up with me!

The next day he called back and said he thought it through again and had changed his mind. He still wanted to date me, but thought we shouldn't spend New Year's Eve together. Justin seemed to think if we spent New Year's Eve together it "meant something" and he clearly wasn't ready for that yet.

So my sister and her husband took pity on me and spent New Year's Eve with me so I wouldn't be alone. In fact, they came over with a big pot of meatballs and spaghetti and we had a nice dinner. Hey, we are Italian after all!

As the relationship with Justin went on, I spent much of my time in an "I don't know" state. I didn't know if I was in love with him. I didn't know if I could get serious about a garbage man. I didn't know if I wanted to be dating him. I just *didn't know*.

Maybe that was apparent to Justin. There were so many times when he would call and say he would be at my house at around 6 p.m. At 8 p.m. the phone would ring again and he was just leaving. I spent a lot of time sitting around waiting. One time, he called at 10 p.m. and was just about to leave. "Don't bother," I said. "It's too late now and I want to go to bed."

On weekends, when he said he was busy or needed to do something for his mother, I didn't find myself overly upset he wasn't coming out. I didn't mind just hanging out by myself with Sophie. Was that how I was supposed to feel in a relationship I was excited about? After nine months of dating, shouldn't I know if I was in love with this person or wanted to build a future with him? But I didn't.

Justin's behavior worsened, so I asked him what was going on. He told me he was finding it hard doing a long-distance relationship and he wasn't sure if he was ready to be in a serious relationship because it seemed as if I was ready to settle down and he just wasn't. That was true. I did want to settle down. I just wasn't sure if I wanted to settle down with *him*.

"I don't find you being passionate about me," he said. "Sometimes I'll pull the being late routine hoping you'll get angry or give me some reaction." The thing is, I didn't really care enough to lay down rules for him. I wasn't letting myself really care much about him because then I would risk getting hurt again. I suppose these antics of his should have bothered me, but they didn't.

Then, in June, I was about to go away for two weeks on a cruise to Alaska with my parents and Justin was going away to Florida to see friends and family to celebrate his birthday. We decided it was a good two weeks apart for us to think about things and see whether or not we wanted to continue the relationship.

While I was away, I didn't miss him at all. Sure, I thought about him and bought him a gift from my travels, but I didn't desperately miss him. "That's not a good sign," I thought.

When I got home, Justin came out to visit me. When I saw him, we kissed and hugged, and I realized I had indeed missed him. He was the one to verbalize it by saying, "You know, I didn't think I really missed you, but now that you are here in front of me, I really did." We had a long talk about our relationship.

"You know, Justin, I really want to try to make this work between us," I said.

"Yes, I do, too, Jane."

"I know I haven't been very accommodating and I will do my best to go into Staten Island to see you more, too," I said. "I can come some days and work from your apartment so we spend more time together. I really think we can make this work."

"Yes, I do, too. I'd like that," he said.

Later, we hugged and kissed and off he went.

Two days later, I got a phone call. Justin didn't seem like himself and when I asked what was wrong, he told me he'd been thinking about it and he didn't want to get serious and he knew I did. I was upset and crying again. I felt like I had finally let my wall down and decided I was going to let someone in. Plus, it took me a long time to look beyond the garbage man status yet now he was treating me like garbage! What was so hard for me to believe was how he could be here two days earlier and tell me he really missed me and wanted to work this out, and then two days later he changed his mind. Okay, this was two times now. I got the message.

Justin and I talked a bit more after the "breakup." A few weeks afterward, I was out on a date with someone else. My phone kept ringing all afternoon. I looked at the caller ID and it was Justin. I certainly wasn't going to answer it in front of my date.

When I got home later, my home phone rang again and it was Justin. "I'm at the mall by your house," he said.

"Why?" I asked.

"I tried to call you earlier, and when you didn't answer, I decided to drive out and see if you were okay," he said. He asked if we could meet for dinner. We did, and it was sad because it was hard to see someone you care about and yet he was still very lost and confused and didn't know what to do with himself. I knew I had to move on.

After I told my friends we had broken up, they all said "I didn't see you with a garbage man anyway. You deserve better."

Justin called me about two months later and wanted to get back together again. I didn't think it was a good idea, so I said no. But the whole experience had really taken its toll.

After that relationship, I finally took Clyde's advice from many years earlier. I realized I needed a break from dating. I took about eight months off. I wasn't into it and was tired of all of the rejection. I decided to focus on me. I really enjoyed spending time with myself. I did things I wanted to do. I began to write this book. I built my business. I made new friends and socialized more. I got back into therapy. I was actually okay with not dating. It was the first time in a very long time I wasn't looking for a man, and it was okay. I began dieting and losing weight. All was right with the world.

A Date With The Red Hat Society

After those eight months were up, I felt a desire to get back in the ring. Stan was perhaps my most unusual first date.

We lived in the same town in New Jersey. He worked in New York as an engineer for a company that worked on the city's major bridges.

Stan was a bit of an odd fellow. Small in stature, he had billed himself on the site as a "renaissance man." For our first date, he invited me to Grounds for Sculpture, an outdoor art museum nearby where he was a docent.

I met him at his house on a very hot summer Sunday morning as he was packing us lunch. Keep in mind this museum had two food outlets — a more expensive restaurant and a café — but he said he never knew the hours of operation of the restaurants so he just thought it safer if we brought our own picnic lunch. I suppose that was a bit romantic — my friends later surmised he was just being cheap.

So we headed over to the sculpture museum and he checked in. He said, "As long as we're here, I might as well guide a tour. You don't mind, do you?" I thought it was a bit odd, but went along with it. Evidently, he needed to put in a certain number of hours per month to keep his docent status, so he figured he'd kill two birds with one stone.

We headed to the outdoor seating area where people can picnic or buy food at the café, and there was a large group of women there who belonged to the ubiquitous "Red Hat Society." Stan announced he was giving a tour and about 30 of these women jumped up to join us.

So for the next 90 minutes, I was joined on my "date" by a bunch of old ladies as Stan gave us a tour — in the sweltering hot sun — of the various sculptures on the grounds. At one point, the ladies asked if I was his wife, and he said dismissively, "No, she's just a friend." I suppose that should have been a clue!

After the tour was over, we sat down at the outdoor eating area and proceeded to have our picnic — ham and cheese sandwiches, iced tea, and grapes. And that was the end of our date.

I don't remember if after that I called him or he called me, but we ended up going out for dinner. I think our initial plans were to go to a jazz festival at an area winery, but it began to rain and so we needed an alternate strategy. I must admit, he was very good about making the plans and taking care of the arrangements.

We had a nice dinner and he drove me home and we chatted for a while in the car, and he didn't make a move, so as I was getting out of the car, I leaned in and gave him a quick kiss on the lips. And that was it ... nothing more from him.

I didn't hear anything from him for quite some time. In the meantime, I was dating some other people, and when those didn't work out, I gave him a call and we met at a Starbucks on Sunday afternoon for coffee. We talked for a while — he was thinking of interviewing for a new job and really seemed to want to stop commuting into the city. The conversation was completely focused on him, and he didn't really have too much interest in what I was doing, nor did he really seem to have too much time to date. Stan always seemed to be coming and going.

After our coffee date, I never called him again and he never called me.

A lot of online dates end up this way. The interaction kind of just fizzles into silence. Nobody was at fault. It just wasn't there.

Labor Day Romance

I had gotten a "wink" from a blond named Patrick in the middle of the summer.

I winked back but hadn't heard anything more from him. Then, in late August, I sent him an e-mail to see what he was up to, and he mentioned he had been away for most of July at a beach house with his brother and then he'd been sick with a bad summer cold. So we made plans to meet for drinks in Lambertville — a very picturesque town on the Delaware River — on the Thursday night before Labor Day weekend.

He was attractive and fun and joked around a lot and we had a good time, although I thought it a bit odd we sat at the bar for about three and a half hours and he never ordered us anything to eat. He told me he worked as a financial officer in a company and it was a pretty easy gig as the department pretty much ran itself. He had definitely achieved a position in life where he was paid well, didn't have to work hard, and had plenty of free time to play. So apparently, he was just cheap.

The next day, he called. "I'd like to see you on Saturday. Could we spend the day together?" he asked. I suggested the sculpture museum (the site of my previous date with Stan and the Red Hat Ladies. Let's face it. In New Jersey there aren't too many cultural things to choose from).

He picked me up and off we went. We spent a very long time touring each and every sculpture, holding hands, touching, and flirting. It felt so good to be with a man who seemed really into me. Someone who wanted to hold my hand. Who would steal a kiss behind an art sculpture. Who would lean in and kiss my cheek. This was how I always dreamed a romantic encounter should be.

After our day out, we decided to go into Princeton for dinner. I recommended a restaurant with outdoor dining and since we had arrived relatively early, there were still some of the coveted outside tables left. But after a quick look around, he decided there must be someplace better to eat, so we walked all over Princeton looking for another restaurant. When there were none to be found (Princeton isn't really known for its fine dining) we ended up back at the first place. Unfortunately, by this time there were no tables left outside or inside so we ended up dining at the bar. Despite the fiasco, we ended up having a really great time. And this time he actually ordered food!

On Labor Day (just two days later), my phone rang at 8 a.m. Lo and behold it was Patrick. "I'd love to spend the day with you today," he tells me. "What are you doing?"

"Um, I didn't really have any specific plans."

"So why don't we meet in New Hope, Pennsylvania and just hang out?" he said.

"Sure, I'd love that," I said.

"Great. Meet me there at 1 p.m. Park in the lot behind the first hotel on your left when you cross the bridge and we'll walk around and decide where to go for a drink," he said.

"Okay, see you then. Bye."

An hour later, he called back and said, "Bring along some of your writing — I would love to see your work."

"Wow, this guy is *really* interested in me," I thought.

We ended up sitting at an outdoor café, and being Labor Day, the town was really hopping. We had appetizers and drinks and then decided to walk around the town. We passed a man selling tickets for the last sightseeing boat down the Delaware River for the summer, so we decided to set sail.

After we arrived back on land, he grabbed my hand and said, "Hey, my friend Todd lives nearby. Why don't we go there for a barbecue?" Interesting, I thought. He wants to introduce me to some of his friends.

"Sure. That sounds great." And off we went.

Instead of ringing the doorbell, he took the key from under the mat and we went in. Evidently his friend was out of town and our barbecue would be a sort of borrow-the-house-and-grill situation. He gave me a tour, we fed the cat, and then he took some steaks out of the freezer and made a nice barbecue. While the food was cooking, things got a bit amorous. We started flirting, teasing, touching, kissing, and before I knew it we were making out on his friend's rumpled bed.

Then we ate, had some wine, and I noticed Patrick started this massive clean-up mission, picking up every trace of everything we had eaten or touched, putting it in a white garbage bag, and taking the bag with us, throwing it into the trunk of his car. I thought this was a bit strange, but didn't say anything. And then we went back into town where my car was parked. We kissed goodbye and went our separate ways after what was a nice day together. (Funny … he never did ask to see those writing samples.)

After about a week, I hadn't heard from him, so as was my MO, I gave him a call.

He seemed very weird and distant. "So when will I see you again next?" I asked. He started hemming and hawing and making excuses about it was getting to be a busy time at work and he really needed to focus on his job. (I wondered what happened to his department pretty much running itself?)

And so I inquired, "What exactly are you saying Patrick? That you don't want to see me anymore?" And he never really came out and said it, but it was clearly the message being delivered. As we were getting ready to hang up the phone, he said "Now, don't be a stranger …"

Don't be a stranger? What the hell? I think he was the strange one! Soon after, he disappeared off the online dating site where I met him. About 10 months later, he was back on and had viewed my profile. But he never made any contact and that was just fine with me. Chalk it up to a quickie summer romance that lasted all of five days.

Even The Long Island Lolita Has A Profile

When you are involved in online dating, you can't help but cheer when a fellow online dater has success ... but Amy Fisher?

Amy Fisher had been dubbed "The Long Island Lolita." As a teenager, she had an affair with an auto body repairman named Joey Buttafuoco and ended up shooting his wife Mary Jo in the face. There was a media frenzy over the case and she served quite a number of years in prison.

Well, one day I was watching *Oprah*, and Amy Fisher was a guest talking about her new book and how she had turned her life around. She was pregnant, and mentioned she had recently gotten married. The kicker was she had met her husband on Match.com!

Hello! Even an infamous convict can meet and marry on Match.com and I can't!

Oprah had asked Amy's husband — who was sitting in the studio audience — if he knew who she was when he first met her and he said he hadn't at the time. (Was he living under a rock or what?)

She recounted how she told him who she was and what had happened to her on their very first date … and he didn't run! Even I never had such bad things to report on a first date. This was very sad indeed.

Don't take this the wrong way. I am very happy Amy Fisher turned her life around. I believe she now works as a columnist for a Long Island newspaper and has two kids. But what is wrong with this picture if she can meet a man online and get married and I can't?

Now this is *really* depressing ….

Fast forward to 2008. I did a search online and found out Amy Fisher's husband filed for divorce, she and Joey were considering doing a reality show together, and her husband sold a sex tape of them to an adult video company against her will! Amy later agreed to promote the video and she and her husband have since reconciled. Life *is* stranger than fiction!

Do Celebrities Date Online?

Knowing Amy Fisher found a husband online made me curious about whether or not other "famous" people, including celebrities, date online.

So I sidled up to my good friend, Google.com, and checked it out.

Believe it or not, I discovered some celebrities have indeed dated online. It must be incredibly difficult for them. Do they post their photos? If they don't, how do they get any traffic?

I have met quite a few men online who write in their profiles they don't have their photo posted because they are "known" in the community or are a "high-profile" individual. I always take that with a grain of salt because I pretty much figure they are either seriously ugly or married or doing something they really shouldn't be doing.

But as I was doing my Google research, I came across an article that said both Joan Rivers and Halle Berry have dabbled in online dating. I guess I am pretty impressed that in her seventies, Joan Rivers would post a profile online complete with photo — nipped and tucked or not! I went to the supposed site she was on and tried a search, but couldn't find her profile.

And imagine a man corresponding with a woman, asking for a photo, and getting one of Halle Berry back? If I were him, I probably wouldn't believe it was truly her, but that would be such a fabulous surprise.

Then again, you have people who wish they were celebrities. One friend sent me an e-mail link to a profile of a guy she was corresponding with who looked like Billy Joel. I checked out the profile, and the photo *was* Billy Joel. I guess the guy thought if women liked Billy Joel, they would like him.

The Princeton University Professor

When I first moved to New Jersey, it seemed I had entered a vast wasteland of blue collar men with limited education. Until I came across Marty.

As it turned out, Marty was a professor at Princeton University. Bingo! I hit the jackpot in the intelligence department.

We met at a local coffee shop in Princeton and when he first walked in, I was a little disheartened by his appearance. He was shorter than I, his skin was a bit pock marked from acne, and it wasn't love at first site. But as we talked and got to know one another, I discovered he had a really appealing personality. He was also a world traveler and had his own import/export business that often took him to the Far East. We had a lot in common with regard to travel, interests, and the like. I was intrigued.

On our first date he took me to a Japanese restaurant for sushi. He was a great conversationalist and we had a really nice time. Marty had been in a 10-year relationship with a woman and had realized it wasn't going to work out half-way through the relationship, but it took him about five years to get out of it. He was also recently on a health kick having lost about 30 lbs. and working out religiously.

He lived in a nearby town and invited me over to see his house and have a drink. It was amazing! The house was beautifully decorated (he was definitely a metrosexual) and in addition to his talents as a professor, businessman, and decorator, he also built his own furniture in his basement woodworking shop. Each room impressed me even more than the last. We then made our way to his office and as I walked in I saw this golden statuette sitting on his desk. A familiar winged creature holding a globe stood before me.

"Is that an Emmy?" I asked, completely dumbfounded.

"Oh, yeah," he replied.

"You have an Emmy?" I repeated.

"Yes."

"A television Emmy?" I clarified. He nodded. "How did you get an Emmy?"

"Oh," he said nonchalantly, "back a number of years ago I consulted on the special effects for the movie *The Day After* helping them do the mushroom cloud and I won an Emmy for that."

Boy, Marty was full of surprises and none of them bad!

On our next date, we went to an Italian restaurant and then came back to hang out at my place for a while. We sat and talked about various things and then all of a sudden the conversation took a bit of an odd turn.

"Listen, Jane. I just want to tell you something," he said.

"Okay? What is it?" I asked a bit apprehensively.

"Well, I really like you."

"I like you, too."

"But I seem to have this pattern when I like a woman, all of a sudden I stop returning her phone calls and e-mails, and pretty much just ignore her," he said.

I took that in, and then said, "Seriously?"

"Yes, I know it's awful. But I wanted to warn you sometimes this happens and I don't want you to take it personally."

"Okay. But if it's a pattern, maybe it's something you want to talk to a shrink about. I'm assuming that can't be working out too well for you," I said.

"He smiled, laughed a bit to himself, nodded, and the conversation moved on to something else. The evening ended on a nice note, but what he said left a residue of unease inside me.

A few days went by and I didn't hear from Marty, which wasn't a surprise since he essentially prepared me for the fact he planned to ignore me. Then, I got an e-mail from him telling me he was going to take my advice and go see a psychiatrist so he was taking himself off of Match.com and was going to stop dating for awhile until he figured himself out.

"Humph!" I thought. I finally found a really interesting, intriguing guy and he decides to follow my advice when I half-jokingly said he should seek therapy for his issue.

I noticed Marty was off the dating site for about six or nine months. When he re-appeared, I e-mailed him to see how things were going and how he was doing. Of course, he ignored me.

The Real Estate Mogul

During one of my desperate periods I came across Jerry's profile.

He seemed to be a little full of himself and pompous, but it was a quiet period and I thought I should expand my horizons.

Jerry said he was pretty well known in my community and owned his own real estate firm. I contacted my sister and brother-in-law, who were long-time residents, and sent them a link to his profile and they called me back laughing.

Evidently, Jerry was a real go-getter, had gone after them many times to list their house, and was in fact quite well known in the community.

Jerry and I agreed to meet for coffee one Sunday afternoon. That morning, I got a call from my sister who told me she and her husband were out to dinner the night before and there was Jerry, also in the restaurant, making out with a blonde woman at the dinner table. A real "get a room" scene, I guess.

If he was dating tons of women, I didn't want to be part of that. I called him up and canceled.

I still laugh every time I drive around town and see a billboard with his photo plastered across it. He might be quite the man about town, but he wasn't the man for me.

The Senior Citizen

Although I had always pictured myself with an older man, when it came to online dating, I had a strong preference to stick close to my own age.

While I'd had a relationship with a man in his early fifties when I was in my thirties (a non-online relationship), the thought of dating a guy in his fifties now that I was this side of 40 seemed more like dating my father. And the truth was most men 50 and over looked older than my dad, which seemed just plain weird.

Robert had contacted me online and was rather persistent. I finally told him I wasn't interested because he was too old for me — his profile listed his age as 55. He kept telling me how he looked younger than his age, and I would be impressed with him, and I should give it a try. So I figured what the heck, although I did do it with some trepidation.

We met for lunch one weekday at a restaurant at a nearby mall. Robert was a real estate developer and investor who had a 5-year-old adopted daughter from his previous marriage.

When I walked into the restaurant and saw him, he was right — he didn't look 55. More like 65. Because of this, right away, I could feel myself shutting down. I had flashbacks to the haircut and glasses guy and just wanted to get out of there! But as so often happens in online dating, you have to sit through the bad first dates, too.

We chatted about a lot of different things.

"You know, Jane, one thing I would really love to do is to take you dancing to some good Frank Sinatra tunes," he said.

"Oh my God," I thought. "You can't be serious." I just sat there and smiled, not knowing what to say. I thought I would die. I could just picture us at an old supper club dancing with all the blue hairs. I mean, my dad loves Frank Sinatra music but even *he* dances to rock and roll.

As we got up from the table at the end of lunch, he totally blindsided me, pulling me toward him and giving me a big bear hug. Completely inappropriate to say the least!

We then left the restaurant and headed into the parking lot.

"May I walk you to your car?" he asked.

I really didn't want him to. What I really wanted was to make a hasty exit. But I suppose the sight of me running from him through the parking lot to my car wasn't very kind.

"Sure, Robert," I said. "That would be nice."

"I'm sorry? What did you say?" he shouted. And as he said that, he proceeded to switch sides with me.

"You need to stay on my left. I don't have hearing in my right ear. I had a brain tumor operation a year or so back and I can't hear a thing on my right side," he said.

I just nodded. Could this date get any worse?

We said our goodbyes and I couldn't wait to make a getaway. The next day, he called me to ask what I thought (again, flashbacks of haircut and glasses guy!), and I very politely worked up the courage to tell him while he was a very nice man, I really didn't feel any chemistry and didn't want to date him.

"Jane, honey, you need to relax and open up! We'd make a great pair! Hey, I was thinking! I could really use your help with PR and marketing on this development deal I'm doing," he said.

"Uh ..."

"And once we spend more time with one another, you'll see we're perfect together!" he said.

I will give him one thing: he was a very persistent and good salesman — he must have excelled at his job — but I finally had to be very blunt.

"Look, Robert," I said, "this is just never, ever going to happen."

The British Fantasy
— Part Deux

Ah, you think I would have learned from my first Brit.

But nooooo, I had to go back for more. What can I say? Like many women I am a sucker for a British accent. And silly me, I thought for sure this guy would be different.

When it comes to online dating, there are quite a number of sites to try. Some are more expensive than others. I naturally assumed the men on the more expensive sites would be more serious about finding a mate.

eHarmony is one of those sites. The only thing is, you don't get to peruse profiles and make a selection. They send you only the men they believe are your perfect matches based upon some "super top secret soul mate algorithm." Personally, I never got it. But lo and behold after quite a dry spell on eHarmony, Stefan showed up on my match list. He was 42 and his photo looked like a young Barry Gibb — who I'd always thought was hot.

He had been living in the U.S. for about 15 years, had been married to an American, and recently divorced. Believe it or not, he had met his ex-wife on the highway — her car had broken down and she had two young children in tow. He'd stopped to help her out, given her a ride home, and then went back to fix the car. Now is that a nice guy or what?

He admitted to being a workaholic during their marriage — dedicated to building his family's company — and as a result, their marriage suffered. He had since sold his interest in the company and was working as Chief Information Officer for the company that had bought it.

We talked on the phone quite a lot — although between his British accent and the poor reception on both our cell phones, it was rather difficult to understand him at times. After quite a period of chatting, I hinted about meeting, and he said he was in no rush and believed things like this took time. So we went on exchanging e-mails and phone calls — he even called me while I was on vacation in Mexico just to say hi. That seemed promising!

After the holidays, I decided it was time to meet and told him so. It turned out we would both be going to meetings in New York City on the same day, and he invited me to lunch at 21. "Nice," I thought. "A classy guy."

The night before, I received an e-mail telling me he had a very important meeting he needed to attend in order to "save the company," as it had been having serious financial trouble, and would have to cancel our date. He profusely apologized and being a businessperson, I understood. The plan was for us to go to this very elegant French restaurant in New Jersey he knew of. It was so exclusive it was only open very limited hours on certain days of the week. So we went about trying to reconcile our schedules.

Once again, he seemed in no rush to meet and I seemed to be the one continually pushing the issue. "Could he be married?"

I thought. Nah, why would someone who is married pay $50 a month to be on this dating service *and* post his photo if he was just looking for a mistress?

Then one Friday afternoon at about 4 p.m., Stefan e-mailed me.

"My dear Jane," his e-mail began. "As I had been telling you, my company is in financial trouble. So as a result, they have decided to let me go. I just found out a few minutes ago and as you can imagine, I am quite in shock. I now need to focus my efforts completely on securing a new position so it is a good probability we will never meet."

Huh? What does losing a job have to do with not being able to find even 60 minutes to go get a cup of coffee? I was continually getting this same lesson over and over again about how men truly compartmentalize their lives ... if their career isn't going well they can't seem to function in any other area.

So that was the last of Stefan — my Barry Gibb fantasy — whom I was looking so very much to meeting. Or so I thought.

About three weeks later, an e-mail arrived in my box from Stefan asking me if I was "still out there."

"Yes," I replied. "But I must say I was a little disappointed at your earlier e-mail which basically blew me off when you lost your job."

"Ah, yes. I apologize," his e-mail said. "I was in terrible shock over having lost my job. It was quite poor behavior. But, alas, as it turned out, I started my own consulting company and have fared quite well over the past few weeks and I am doing better financially than when I worked for the company. So if you are still out there, I would like to meet you. Please give me a second chance if you will?"

"Sure, why not," I thought. My curiosity got the better of me!

We made plans to meet the next Sunday for brunch. Where would we meet? Being a recent transplant from New York I didn't know much beyond my own neighborhood, and I thought it only fair we meet midway between where he lived and where I lived. He selected a restaurant about 45 minutes from my house and even went so far as to MapQuest the directions for me. On Friday afternoon, he called to confirm: Sunday at 12 noon.

"I'll wait for you right inside the restaurant at the hostess desk," he said.

For some reason, with all of my dating escapades — undoubtedly having met over 200 men — I still got nervous every time I met someone face-to-face for the first time. My neighbor, Shelley, insisted she was going to do my makeup for me to help me look great and boost my confidence.

That morning, I woke up to torrential rains and a weird feeling in my stomach that I really didn't want to meet this guy and wasn't in the mood for dating. I would have preferred sleeping late and cuddling with my dog, Sophie. But I got up and put myself together — changing outfits a million times it seemed. You'd think I was meeting Barry Gibb himself the way I was acting. And then I went to Shelley's to have my makeup done. A 10-minute makeup job ended up taking more like 25, and so I left the house late.

I was still not in the mood to meet him for whatever reason. I was insecure, and I was late. As I pulled out of my driveway, I called his cell phone to tell him I was running late, but wanted to assure him I would indeed be there. No answer.

The weather was horrible, and the drive slow going. At the time I was supposed to be there, I called his cell phone again. No answer. "Hi Stefan, this is Jane," I said. "I just wanted to let you know I am running a bit late, but I *am* on my way and I should be there very soon."

I had to park four blocks away and run in the pouring rain to the restaurant. I arrived only 15 minutes past our appointed meeting time, bolted through the door, and began my search for Barry Gibb. He was nowhere in sight.

"Excuse me," I said to the hostess, out of breath. "Is there a dark-haired man with a beard waiting for a guest?"

"No ma'am," said the hostess. "There haven't been any single guests at all this morning. Only groups. But feel free to walk the restaurant if you like to see if you can find your guy."

"Thanks," I replied and began my circuit of the restaurant.

I didn't see him. "I guess he is running late as well," I thought.

I called Shelley to give her the scoop and she advised me to wait at least an hour. After all, rain can wreak havoc on traffic and he had quite a long drive as well. I waited until about 12:45 p.m. and called his cell phone again. No answer. "He's not coming," I thought. "And I hope he wasn't in an accident."

It seemed the torrential rains wouldn't end! I white-knuckled it home and Shelley met me for a bite to eat at our local diner. To this day, I have never heard from Stefan. Not a phone call, not an e-mail, no carrier pigeon, nothing.

In all of my 43 years, it was the first time I had ever been stood up. And it felt pretty crappy. I don't know if he was on a power trip, chickened out, or just plain forgot. I guess I'll never know.

Stefan, if you are out there and reading this — your name has not been changed to protect the innocent and I hope you know what a shit you are!

Recycling A Relationship

About 10 months after Justin and I broke up — the day after Easter to be exact — I checked my Blackberry and there was an e-mail waiting from you know who.

For a minute, my heart stopped. "What does he want?" I thought. He was just checking in to say hi and wanted to see how I was doing, how my family was doing, and if I had a good Easter. So I responded. And we begin a nice, safe e-mail correspondence back and forth every few days.

Justin told me he had finally started taking flying lessons again. While we were together, he had talked and talked about wanting to get his pilot's license, but he never did anything about it in a consistent way. Finally, he had taken some action and was working toward it! Could this mean a new career? One actually out of the garbage industry? Imagine!

And then it happened. He asked me if he could take me out to dinner. *What to do. What to do.*

After much thought, I agreed. Mind you, in the back of my head I was thinking, "Does he want to get back together? Do I? Can I really get over the garbage man thing? Do I miss him? Could this work again? Am I crazy for going back for more?" It's amazing how many things can run through your mind and how many conversations you can have with yourself about all of the possibilities out there. My mind was working overtime trying to figure out what to do.

Sure, every woman wants a man who dumped her to come back and profess his love for her and to admit leaving her was the biggest mistake he had ever made. I was flattered he wanted to come take me out to dinner, but for all I knew, that might be all it was — just two people going out for dinner.

Of course, I dressed up and made sure I looked very sexy. I was growing my hair long so I could donate it to Locks of Love and I knew Justin loved my hair long. (For the record, I looked fantastic!)

He came over to my house, and we broke the tension by playing with Sophie for a few minutes. I picked a romantic restaurant in Lambertville along the Delaware River. We had a really nice dinner and we talked. I talked about what I had been up to. He talked about what he had been up to. We laughed about some of our dating shenanigans and what we were looking for in someone. I stuck with what I had said in the first place: I wanted someone who was dedicated to their career, who was driven and ambitious, who wanted to settle down and was ready for a relationship. And he told me how he had really gotten himself together.

"Jane, I have to tell you, I've really changed," he said. "I'm committed to getting my pilot's license. I think it is something I can be really good at and maybe make a career out of it."

I had to admit I was attracted to him once again. And this time around, he even put the napkin on his lap and knew which silverware to use. He had come a long way in a year. I kept waiting for him to bring up something about him and me, but he never did.

I was getting anxious to learn why he'd called this dinner meeting.

"So … I'm glad you called," I said. "I have to admit I have had times when I thought about you and me."

"Yeah, Jane, me too," he said. "I've been thinking about us a lot, too."

It was so nice to finally be wanted, for him to be clear. And *finally*, we were moving past the garbage man thing. But in the back of my mind, I could hear all of the naysayers. I knew my friends would be shocked if Justin and I got back together, as would my family. In fact, I knew my family would be furious. My dad never liked him and always said I could do much better than a garbage man, and my sister and brother-in-law thought it was terribly wrong I would pay my way every time we went out. My sister was also of the mindset "He dropped you twice … why would you go back for more?"

"But he's changed," I thought. My mind began to race back and forth between the possibilities and the past.

I had to agree with my sister on one front. So much so I let him pay for dinner that night, and it wasn't cheap! We came back to my house and hung out on the couch for a long time watching TV. "Is he going to make the first move?" I thought. We were both uncomfortable and nervous. And then he kissed me, and soon thereafter we were in bed … and it felt like nothing had changed. The 10 months we had been apart had just melted away.

The next day, he made breakfast and we sat out on my deck off the kitchen.

"I know I am really jumping the gun here, Justin, but I think it's important I make myself really clear about where I stand if we are even considering getting back together," I said.

"Yes, I know, Jane. I agree," he said.

"For starters, I am looking to get married. I am not into casual dating anymore," I said, anticipating the usual standoffish response.

"Yes, I know. I'm ready to settle down, too, Jane. If things are to work out between us."

"And I would never live in Staten Island. So you would need to live here in New Jersey," I said. I glanced over at him to gauge his reaction. He didn't flinch.

"That's fine. I'm really getting tired of the traffic and noise on Staten Island, anyway. It's really nice out here, Jane. I could definitely see myself living out here."

"But would you be able to stand the commute to your job?" I asked.

"Well, officially I couldn't say I lived out here, because to work for the city, you're required to live there. I would have to use my Mom's address or something. But yes, I could do that," he said.

"Why don't you just leave the Sanitation Department once and for all? What is keeping you there?" I asked, and I could feel my old frustrations coming up. He'd rather commute all the way from New Jersey to Staten Island to pick up people's stinky garbage than get a different job?

"Well, for one thing I get really great benefits," he said. "You're self-employed, so if we got married, you could have my benefits. And I would have benefits for life — even after I retired. Just think about it. After about eight more years, I can retire with at least a half pension and we would always have money coming in and full benefits and we could start whatever business we wanted. That is a much bigger benefit than most people have."

"Hmmm ..." I thought. His reasoning actually made sense. And he had obviously given a lot of thought to our future. I finally made peace with the garbage man status.

For weeks after, we talked about everything. Did we want kids? What did he want to eventually do as a career? I made myself very clear about everything I expected from him in this relationship and he said he understood. We had started on a new footing and it was good. It all felt right. And this time around he was different. He came out when he said he would come out. He introduced me to his friends. He surprised me with a long weekend away to see his sister. And he paid for every meal whenever we went out. We talked about the future and it seemed promising. I was happy, and I was definitely falling in love with him.

We had settled into a really good rhythm. And I have to say, it wasn't easy for me. I had never let someone in so much. I let him see me when I wasn't feeling well. I let him see my closet was a mess and my underwear drawer wasn't organized. And for the first time, I really felt I could just be myself with this man. I didn't need to put on airs or be someone I was not. And it was okay. He didn't judge me and he didn't run. "Wow," I thought. "This might really work out."

Overall, the relationship was good. We spent every weekend together and had a fabulous time whether we were shopping in Wal-Mart or going to a winery for a romantic weekend. One night we were in his house and he was showing me old family movies and his sister called. At the end of the conversation he said, "I love you, too."

"So you do have that word in your vocabulary?" I said.

He smiled and said "You know I love you, Jane."

"I love you, too," I said and then we hugged. It was the first time a man had ever told me he loved me! Why didn't I see fireworks? Maybe I was in a bit of shock. What now? Would my life be forever perfect now that a man loved me? (If only life were that easy.)

A few weeks later, I asked, "So when *did* you know you loved me?"

"I've always loved you, Jane," he said. Wow. So how come he never said it before? We women are just never happy, are we? And my therapist had told me a few weeks before I had to accept the fact I might be with someone who just cannot communicate his feelings.

Not long thereafter, my business became very busy. I was working night and day and was about to leave on a business trip to Guatemala. I was so stressed out I developed a cold sore on my lip. I was supposed to leave on a Friday morning. The day before I was due to fly, a big terrorism scare happened in London and they banned all liquids on the planes. My trip was postponed, and I was to fly out the following week instead. I called Justin and asked if he wanted to come out for the weekend and he told me he had already made plans with his buddies. I understood.

We spoke over the weekend and it turned out he hadn't really done much with his buddies. The real reason he didn't want to come out was he was afraid of catching my cold sore. A germ phobic garbage man! Interesting!

Apparently this cold sore thing really had him freaked out — especially since he did a little research and learned a Herpes simplex virus caused the cold sore.

The next day, Justin told me he went to the doctor and had a Herpes test and all of these other sexually transmitted disease tests. How ignorant could he be to think the Herpes virus that caused cold sores is the same virus as genital Herpes?

I was at once stunned and completely freaked out and furious because he had assumed I had all of these sexually transmitted diseases and wasn't telling him! All because of a stupid cold sore. It turned out he was positive for the Herpes virus that causes cold sores and the doctor told him he probably had it since he was a kid because he had had the chicken pox and it was doubtful he had gotten it from me. But you would have thought he was told he had AIDS or something!

He started to act really weird after that. "I'm not really sure I could live out in New Jersey," he said. "And what would I do with my mother? If I moved in with you, would she move in, too?"

Did I just hear that right?

"No," I said. "We could get her an apartment nearby if you want."

He was starting to back pedal on all of the things we had discussed. "Sure, I can live in New Jersey," he'd said. "Sure, I want to settle down with you." And suddenly he wasn't so sure anymore. "Here we go again!" I thought.

I was stressed out, sick of the runaround and wanted to get to the bottom of this, so I called him. "Justin, what the heck is up with you?" I said. "Why are you making such a federal case out of a stupid cold sore?"

"I don't know, Jane. I just am."

"You know, I have to leave on a business trip tomorrow and I'm very stressed out with all the work I have to do. And the fact I have to travel with all of these terrorism warnings is scaring the shit out of me. I could use some support here! What is going on with you?"

"I don't know what to say, Jane. I just can't help myself," he said.

I hung up the phone on him. So self-absorbed. And he didn't even wish me a safe trip. What a jerk!

Even so, I hated leaving things unsettled. While I was away, I kept calling him but we just couldn't connect. I hated being away and having my relationship hanging in the balance. We played phone tag the whole time I was gone although I really don't think he was that intent on actually reaching me.

When I got home I thought I would at least find a "welcome home" message on my voice mail from him, but there was nothing. I waited the entire next day and he didn't call. Finally, I called him and left a message. Two hours later, my phone rang. "I was afraid to answer the phone because I was afraid you would yell at me again," he said. Whatever!

Whenever I tried to talk to him about his behavior and his lack of support, he was tired or didn't want to talk about it. I was getting nowhere fast and it was really starting to bother me. Two days later I was to leave for Washington, D.C. for a day trip. As I rode the train down to D.C., my anger grew.

I picked up my trusty Blackberry and sent him a message: "I'm done." Clearly he didn't want to be in a relationship anymore and I was tired of the way he was treating me. An immediate feeling of relief and peace poured over me ... particularly since our relationship had caused a big rift between my dad and me.

He was furious we were back together and was barely speaking to me. I felt like I had to choose between my father and Justin, and it wasn't an easy choice. And my sister and her husband were also against it. Perhaps without Justin, my life overall would just be easier, I thought.

I arrived home from Washington, D.C. that night about 7:30. I just felt like finding something to eat and going to bed early. Shelley called and said she was going out for ice cream and asked if I wanted any. "Sure," I said. "Chocolate, chocolate chip sounds perfect right about now."

About 20 minutes later, the doorbell rang, and I went to get my ice cream. There standing on my stoop was Justin. I have to tell you — I really just wanted the ice cream. It was quite a disappointment to see him instead. "Can we talk?" he asked. Shelley was pulling in the driveway and saw what was happening. She gave me a look of disbelief. Of course she knew the entire story.

What was I going to do? He had driven all the way out from Staten Island. I let him in.

"I'm sorry, Jane," he said. "I want to build a life with you. I really do. I don't know what's wrong with me." His eyes filled with tears. He held my hand. (Don't get me wrong. I was still pissed.)

"Do you want to go for a walk?" he asked. We took Sophie for a walk, but I kept my distance. He told me he'd rented a movie for us to watch. (Boy, he was sure of himself, wasn't he?) I told him I was tired and wanted to go to bed, and so we did. To *sleep*, by the way.

The next day we slept late and I had a friend coming from out of town for a visit. I invited Justin to come along for dinner but he said he knew it was a girl's night out so he stayed home. He was quiet and depressed and lacked enthusiasm. He ended up staying four days in my house as he was on vacation that week. It was Mike all over again: I couldn't take him just lying around! I sent him to check out some flight schools in the area. As it turned out, he found one nearby he really liked and he enrolled. At least he was back on track with that.

And then on Friday he said he needed to go back and do some things for his mother and get himself ready to return to work. As I got ready for work, he sat in the chair in my bedroom and looked around for a long while, making no effort to move. I was anxious to get down to my office and start working. He came down to the living room, and as he was packing up his stuff, he knelt down on the floor and started petting Sophie and playing with her. He stayed down there petting her for a really long time not saying a word. Something didn't feel right. Then he kissed me, hugged me, and said he would call me later. He did, and we talked briefly because he was having dinner with a friend.

That weekend my sister came to stay for a girl's weekend since her husband was out of town. We went out for a really nice decadent dinner and while she was in the ladies room before we left the restaurant, I checked my Blackberry and there was an e-mail from Justin.

"I know you're going to be mad at me," it said. "But I just can't do this. I don't know what's the matter with me, but I'm not ready for this kind of a relationship. I need to take a step back and date more casually."

"You have to be kidding!" I thought. Not again! This was the fourth time he had pulled this. I was furious. I was sad. I was feeling so many different emotions. I tried to call him, but he didn't answer the phone.

And so I sent him an e-mail: "NEVER call me again. NEVER write to me again. NEVER come out to see me again!"

I knew I couldn't trust him or believe anything he said to me. And that was the God's honest truth. Even if he dropped to one knee with a diamond engagement ring professing his love, I would never be sure if he would actually make it down the aisle.

And there I was, alone again. Another failed relationship.

A few months after Justin and I broke up I took a writing workshop. It was meant to inspire my creativity, but in reality, it helped me heal. The workshop facilitator — a very inspirational writer named Nancy Slonim Aronie — encouraged healing through writing. She would start out each exercise and give us a sentence to write from. This particular assignment was to "write about a time you weren't invited." Here is what I wrote:

I WASN'T INVITED ... to be a part of his life any longer. Suddenly, there was no place for me in his heart.

We had our ups and downs, our breakups and makeups, our questions and concerns. He was younger. I was older. We lived in two different states. Our lives were completely different. And yet our paths became one.

Something drew us to each other — a sense of safety, a place of comfort, a passionate desire. I was beautiful to him. I found myself at peace. I could be "me." He saw me undone, unglued, and uncompromising. And he didn't run, but instead, came back for more.

I experienced a man of honor. A man of kindness. A man of quiet strength. He was everything and nothing I wanted him to be. And I couldn't get enough.

But there was always uncertainty. Is he "the one"? Am I ready to settle down with her? Can I really spend the rest of my life with this person — or was there someone better out there? Was one ever REALLY sure? I was in a perpetual state of "I don't know." And I suppose, he was too.

He left. And came back. Left again. And came back. But I was through, emotionally exhausted, done with it all. And then I missed him. And then I grieved. And then I moved on ... to a place where alone was okay and I took great joy in rediscovering me. I no longer needed to be part of a couple. Singlehood was finally bearable. Singlehood — dare I say it — was actually fun. I could breathe again.

Ten months later he returned. I was lonely. I was weak. I went back for more. It was sheer bliss. I received flowers, compliments, and attention. I met his family, his friends, his co-workers. We talked about kids, living arrangements, careers. We shared dreams, hopes, laughter, and tears. When he held me, all was right with the world. And there was no place else I wanted to be.

And then he told me he loved me. That he had always loved me. That he wanted to build a life with me.

And the next day, he was gone.

The Dry Spell

Right after Justin broke up with me, I vowed I was going to show *him*. I was putting myself right back on the dating market.

The truth was, I had never really taken myself *off*. In fact, just a few weeks before Justin and I broke up for the final time, I was chatting with another man I was planning to meet. I ended up canceling the date the day after Justin came back professing his love. We were supposed to meet on the day Justin sent me that final e-mail breaking up with me. Karma, I suppose.

I felt like a horrible shit I was planning a date with this guy. But my friends said I didn't have a ring on my finger and I should date around and be sure before I committed myself. Actually I had gone out on another date with a non-online man the week after Justin and I got back together. I don't know how people juggle men. I felt horrible doing what I did to both guys. Luckily, I guess, the date didn't work out.

And so I was back full force into dating. I winked at people online. I sent e-mails. I got no replies. No interest. Nothing. No one was winking at me, writing me, or even looking at my profile. It was an honest-to-goodness dry spell. And I felt horrible.

My feelings were compounded by the fact my two neighbors, who were both doing online dating and had never had much luck, were both seeing people they met online. One relationship was so serious they were talking about moving in together. And that sent me into a frenzy of jealousy and anger. She'd been married once already. She had her chance! Now it's my turn. Why didn't all my dating efforts pay off? I was so angry and upset and all I was hearing about from my friends were great things about their boyfriends and how great the sex was and how nice it was to fall asleep in a man's arms. Everything I'd had, but lost.

I fell into a deep depression. I even found myself avoiding my friends because I didn't want to hear about their relationships. Every one of my single friends with whom I had commiserated for years about the trials and tribulations of online dating were now matched up! Everyone except for me. Yes, the pity party was in full swing.

Back to square one, yet again!

Express Dating

It was time for a new plan of attack!

I widened my geographic search area online to a 50-mile radius and away I went. This time I wanted someone who was successful in their career and made a good living. I was tired of dating men with career issues who didn't feel ready to settle down yet.

And so I spied Parker. He was good looking in an understated, yet almost rugged way, and I found him attractive. I winked at him and he e-mailed me right back. He was a police detective who served warrants. We e-mailed a few more times and then he sent me his phone number and asked me to call him. I never do that. I feel like I have to get to know someone a bit over e-mail before I'm going to talk with them. But I suppose I was feeling desperate and wanted to get something going. So I called.

He was nice, seemed to have a bit of a shtick going, and as it turned out, he was leaving on a Caribbean cruise the next day by himself — or so he said. He jokingly asked if I wanted to go, and I said "maybe next time." We had made tentative plans to meet the week after he got back and he said he might try and call me from his cruise during the week just to prove his sincerity. I thought it was a little strange.

The next day, I was getting a manicure when my phone rang. It was Parker. He had just landed in Miami and was about to board the cruise ship but wanted to call and tell me he was thinking of me. And he wanted to tell me he thought I was beautiful. Okay, it was flattering, but a little bit weird as we had talked for only about 20 minutes previously.

A few days later, I was at the office when my cell phone rang. Guess who? I didn't answer. When I checked my voice mail, his message said he was in St. Thomas and he was calling to tell me he missed me. Missed me? I've never even *met* you. "Okay, this is officially weird," I thought. "Doesn't he have anything better to do on vacation than call me?" And would you believe just two hours later he called again? This time I picked up. He said he missed me and just wanted to say hi. I think he wanted me to say I missed him too, but that was impossible … I didn't even know this man, let alone miss him.

When he got back, I was away on a business trip and my cell phone rang during a dinner with my client. I glanced at the caller ID, and you'll never guess who it was!

I was starting to feel more than a little weird about this. So I sent him an e-mail and told him I thought it was very premature for him to be calling me from his cruise and telling me he missed me when we barely know each other.

When he called the next day he said, "I'm 42 years old. I know enough not to fall in love with a woman I haven't even met yet. But I do miss you." And then he kept joking about it throughout the phone call telling me he missed me and I was beautiful. I ended the conversation pretty quickly, feigning exhaustion. The next day I sent him an e-mail just saying I wasn't into it anymore and just wasn't feeling the chemistry.

I never heard from him again, which was fine with me. You'd think a police detective, of all people, would be familiar with stalker behavior!

And They Say Women Can't Make Up Their Minds!

After The Perfect Man, Stefan, Justin, and all the others, I was very intent on finding a man who knew what he wanted and was secure in himself and his success.

A neighbor had talked me into checking out a site called www.plentyoffish.com. It was a free dating site, and I had started to believe you got what you paid for. But I poked around, and most of the men on there were looking for afternoon liaisons or one-night stands. I was about to take my profile off the site when Harry contacted me.

His profile and his photos struck me. He had three great shots I found really attractive. His eyes were very expressive and his smile was warm. He also had a photo posed in a garden with flowers and it was very nice and comforting. And he seemed warm and genuine. He was a landscape designer (thus the photo posed in the pretty garden!) and his profile said he was looking for a serious relationship, and he was not into one-night stands, serial daters, or anything like that. He sent me this lovely note:

"Hi there. I read your profile and while I may not fit everything you are looking for, I hope you will give me a chance.

I looked at your photos and found you to be a very beautiful and compelling woman. Your eyes are beautiful and your smile warms my heart. I hope you will give me the chance to get to know you.

My name is Harry, and I am a very grounded, family-oriented person. I have my own landscaping business and while I don't make as much as you stated you prefer in your profile, I do pretty well for myself. I also clean up well. And I am not as tall as your profile requested, but I am taller than you — at five feet, eight inches tall. I hope you will give me a chance because I am quite attracted to you and think we could have a good time getting to know one another."

I found myself very attracted to him as well.

We proceeded to e-mail back and forth for a few days and the "coincidences" started to become uncanny. We were both of Italian descent. He had just lost his mother to Alzheimer's and my mother was currently struggling with the disease. His mother's name was Nancy, the same as a sister of mine who passed away before I was born.

When we finally had a phone conversation, I was struck by the deep feelings of this man. When he told me how he held his mother the day she died, it nearly brought me to tears. I could tell by the tone of his voice and the gentle breaks here and there he was near tears as well.

We talked for nearly two hours and had made plans to meet a few days later. For the first time in a long time, I had butterflies about meeting a man. Wow, that felt really good!

I didn't hear from him the next day, but the following day I received an e-mail that completely caught me by surprise. It said he wasn't sure he was ready for a relationship, he'd been crying all week and was struggling with his mother's death, and he was fresh out of a relationship (oops — I guess he forgot to mention that) so he thought all he could offer me was friendship.

Hello? Is this the same man I just spoke to two nights prior? What is this, the Twilight Zone?

So I sent him an e-mail back saying frankly I was surprised, I had no interest in meeting if all he wanted to do was be friends, and I found him to be a little lost.

He replied the next day.

"Hi Jane," his e-mail began. "I had a feeling you would probably take my e-mail wrong. What I meant to say was I am not ready for an immediate serious relationship, but I would like to date and slowly see what happens if it is okay with you?"

"I don't recall asking you to set a wedding date anytime soon," I thought. I started to realize here was yet another mixed-up guy and I was getting flashbacks to Justin. I didn't want to go through this again.

As lonely as I was, I realized it was better not to push it. There were red flags all over the place.

At my next therapy session, I asked Clyde, "Why do I always attract the confused, non-committal types?" He said to me, "You attract the confused men. Other women attract the cheaters or the con men." And we both agreed it could be worse.

When Worlds Collide

There have been a few times when the online dating world and the real world have collided, and let me tell you, it couldn't be more awkward.

One day I was on Match.com. You can look to see who has checked out your profile, and I would check this periodically. I stared aghast at the screen. The weird guy who was the building manager of my townhouse community had checked out my profile!

Mort was a balding guy who drove a rust bucket car and really made my skin crawl. He gave off a creepy vibe I can't quite explain. I always felt like he was undressing me with his eyes or staring at me just a bit too intently. The thought that someone I knew and had to deal with on a semi-frequent basis about leaks in my roof now knew I was single and dating online freaked me out. He had read all the personal things about me, like I love spooning and bubble baths. It creeped me out.

Part of the benefit of online dating was I could be completely anonymous. And in a city like New York, chances were pretty slim I would actually meet one of these people on the street by chance. I guess I didn't realize New Jersey was such a small world! Thank goodness he left the townhouse community not long thereafter, so I didn't have to worry about that anymore.

And then one day, I was hosting a grand opening event for a client of mine who was taking over management of a hotel in Princeton. The local newspaper was sending over a photographer to cover the event, and when the man showed up he looked incredibly familiar to me, but I just couldn't place him. I felt funny asking where I knew him from, so I let it go.

A few weeks later, when I was surfing online, I come across his photo!

I sent him an e-mail and said hello. Surprisingly, he remembered me right away. I thought he was sexy, so I asked him if he wanted to meet for coffee and he told me he had just rekindled a romance with an old flame and was going offline. Timing is everything, I suppose, and then his profile disappeared.

A few months later, I saw his profile back online again and contacted him. Apparently, like most of us, he had remembered why he had broken off the relationship with the old flame the first time and was back in the online dating world again.

I invited him out for coffee yet again, but he told me he didn't think we were cut out for one another. He said I was more the executive, straight-laced type and he had piercings and tattoos in "places I could only imagine."

I was a bit disappointed, but didn't take offense.

I saw him a few months ago at an event at the hotel again. We've created a nice working relationship and we chit-chat about our online dating escapades now.

My new neighbor next door is also online. I had known he was there for quite awhile, but after hearing about him and how poorly he treated women from his ex (she and I are friends and he bought her out of her house next door to mine), that was a "no go" zone. After he moved in, I saw he had checked out my profile. Once again, I feel a tad exposed. For some reason, it's okay to have my "life" out there to people I figure I will never meet, but when it's someone you see every day, it is truly a weird feeling.

The Sports Writer

One day, a newspaper writer contacted me through one of the sites.

"Ah, a kindred spirit," I thought. He wrote for a number of area newspapers as a columnist. Since I have written for magazines, I felt like we might have a lot in common. He had always worked as a freelance writer and I was impressed he had raised a family and worked his entire career (I think he was in his late 40s) as a writer. His focus was sports. (Not my favorite thing, but writing is writing.)

After a few e-mails, we spoke on the phone, and the conversation was extremely strained. Usually, I give great phone and can get anyone into a comfortable, light-hearted conversation. But there was no spark or chemistry. He asked if I wanted to meet at the local Starbucks for a coffee and I decided to give him a break as he was probably nervous.

We met the week before Thanksgiving. He was definitely a "man's man" and not who I was used to dating. A little rough around the edges. Yes, I realize I dated a garbage man and a ferry boat captain, but those were exceptions. Really. My usual man was a polished, NYC executive type. (How exciting a book would it be to only recount dates with guys in pinstripe suits?) Anyway, he was born in Pennsylvania and had spent most of his time between Pennsylvania and New Jersey. He hadn't been to Europe or out of the country (I'm talking not even Canada and Mexico here), and in this day and age — and since I work in the travel industry — I found that unfathomable.

We chatted, but it was a stilted conversation and I guess I tend to put my journalism training to good use in these first-date situations by asking questions that cannot be answered with a simple yes or no, and getting my date to talk about himself.

"So what are you doing for Thanksgiving next week?" I asked, hoping to start some ongoing dialogue.

"Probably nothing. Will have my kids with me and we'll probably just go to the diner for a quick bite."

"Oh," I answered. I couldn't relate to this. In my family — and with most people I know — Thanksgiving is a big holiday and getting together to enjoy a big, elaborate meal is the main part of the occasion. So after about an hour or so, we said our goodbyes and went on our merry way. I didn't think much about him afterward. I just didn't detect a spark. I guess my fantasy of dating a writer and the reality were two different things. But I might have gone on a second date with him, just to be sure.

Fast forward some four months later. The Sports Writer left me a voice mail one day telling me he was meeting friends in northern New Jersey for dinner and wondered if I wanted to meet him afterward.

Hello? I don't hear from you in four months and then you call out of the blue and want me to meet you on the same day in a few hours ... and for what? After you already have dinner with someone else? There was no, "Sorry I haven't spoken to you in four months." It was as if it was only a few days after our coffee date.

Needless to say, I never responded. He must have gotten the message as he hasn't called back since. Memo to men: Don't keep us waiting.

Some Dates Just Come Up Short

There are times when you meet a guy and nothing is really wrong with him, but for whatever reason, you just don't click.

Brad and I corresponded online for a bit and then agreed to meet one night for a drink at a pub near my house. I pulled up in the parking lot and caught sight of him sitting in a pickup truck so I went over to say hello.

He opened the door, got out of the truck, and stepped down next to me. When I say stepped down, I mean he *really* stepped down. More like hopped. It's a wonder his feet could hit the pedals. His profile said he was 5' 8". There really are a lot more short guys out there than I had ever imagined, or maybe I just never noticed them until I started dating!

I hoped he hadn't seen the look of utter shock on my face. I gathered my composure and we went into the bar, sat on some stools, and ordered drinks. Brad was a nice guy. He wore his head shaved which looked sexy on some guys, but in this case, didn't really do anything for me.

There was nothing wrong, scary, or weird about Brad. He seemed comfortable with himself, his career, and his life. We chatted politely and ordered some appetizers, but it became a bit harder and harder to keep the conversation going. It's amazing how sometimes you just click with somebody and can't shut up and other times there's nothing there. He didn't turn me off in the least either.

After about an hour or so, we decided to end the night and said polite goodbyes in the parking lot. We both knew we would not be seeing one another again and thankfully neither of us said, "Would you like to do this again?"

Who knows why this happens? But I think the wise thing is not to force something that is just not there.

The Truth Hurts

In online dating, what you see is not always what you get.

Once I was contacted by a man who didn't have a photo posted. I told him if he wanted me to consider him, he would need to send or post a photo. He sent me one and I wasn't really attracted, but then again, it wasn't a very good quality snapshot either. So I asked if he had another photo. And he sent one. It was clearer, but didn't improve his looks much. But as we got to know one another a bit more via e-mail his personality was winning me over. And then we made tentative plans to meet for coffee over the weekend. I called and left a message at a friend's house where he was staying for the weekend. He called me when I was in the shower and left a message on my cell phone. When I picked up the voice-mail I was in shock. He was an art buyer for an ad agency and yet he sounded unprofessional, rough around the edges, and very effeminate. Pick your turnoff!

"Now what should I do?" I thought. I had no clue. I didn't return the call because I was trying to figure out how to deal with it. The more I kept playing the message over and over, the more I realized I just couldn't see myself dating or living with that voice every day. Later that night, he called again. I couldn't bring myself to answer the phone. "Let's see how he sounds on this next message," I thought. I listened. Oh no ... just as bad. Yikes! What the heck was I going to do?

A friend said I should tell him I'm taking a break from dating. But he would still see me online, and plus, I didn't really want to lie. The next day I got an e-mail from him saying, "Hi Jane. I got your message. You have such a very pretty voice. I really cannot wait to talk to you to hear that voice again." ("Wish I could say the same," I mused.)

I thought about it for a minute, and decided to be honest. I replied I appreciated his compliment, but to be honest, his voice didn't really turn me on and I wished him the best of luck. My friend chastised me, saying it was a horrible thing to do. Granted, I was feeling in a shitty mood; however, I just didn't feel like creating a long, drawn-out story.

Online dating is the complete antithesis of "real world" dating. In the real world, you see someone in a bar, across a room at a party, or in a supermarket, and you make eye contact and you realize there is some attraction there. So when the person actually asks you out, there are no surprises. You have probably chatted a bit about the weather or the party, so you know there is interest there. But in online dating, you are literally flying blind. First you have to see if you like the person's photo. Okay, he's attractive (assuming the photo is an accurate portrayal, of course), then you move down to their basic profile — what type of education he has, what he does for a living, how much money he makes, what his marital status is, if he has kids, blah, blah, blah. Then you start corresponding, and if you hit it off, you usually talk on the phone. Okay, conversation went well, let's meet. So there are a lot of steps you need to pass before you actually get to the *okay, we like each other, let's date and see where this goes* stage.

I suppose someone's mood and mental state has a lot to do with things as well. If I've been broken up with or treated badly by a man, I pity the poor guy who contacts me next. Sometimes I will bait them and tear them to pieces if they are still corresponding with me, even after my first few snotty responses.

One man contacted me who wasn't bad looking, but he made under $25,000 and was 44 years old. He had just graduated college with a degree in screenwriting, but was now working as a bellman. Hello? You are 44 years old! It gave new meaning to the words late bloomer! I know it sounds harsh, but I don't think I need to settle for someone who can't at least match what I make.

I really tried to avoid being harsh. When the screenwriting bellman contacted me, I politely replied I didn't think we were a match and I wished him the best of luck. But he kept coming back for more. "Why aren't we a match?" he asked. "I think we have a lot in common." I'm sorry, but if you're going to keep asking for it, sooner or later I am going to deliver the truth … harsh or not.

The Flying Dutchman

Here's somebody new!

I was surfing on Match.com one day in my new and improved search criteria (divorced, no kids, within a 35-mile radius, over $100,000 income) when I came across a fresh profile. He looked attractive and we seemed to have a lot in common. I winked at him. He wrote me. We continued to write back and forth all Sunday afternoon and then planned a date for the following Sunday at a bookstore.

I got there early, and he was already there. Good sign! He didn't look exactly like his picture, but I could pick him out well enough. On paper, he was very appealing ... European (Dutch and Portuguese descent), living here in the U.S. for about 12 years, divorced, no kids, and a good job, liked to travel, seemingly normal. How refreshing! We had a great conversation about travel, jobs, cultures, work, dining, movies, books, and I had a good time. As he walked me to my car, he asked for my phone number, which he put right into his cell phone. Another good sign! When I got home, there was already an e-mail waiting from him. "Ready for a date?" it asked. I was. Finally, no games. I didn't have to wait around to see if he would call or analyze every second of the date to see if we hit it off. Or wonder if he liked me or thought I was too fat. This was real progress.

For our first real date, he took me to one of the nicest and most romantic restaurants in the area. It was his favorite place, and I was glad he shared it with me. We had a really nice time and ended up closing the restaurant. He walked me to my car, and we stood talking for a while. I wondered if he was going to kiss me. And finally he did. And it was very nice. His lips were quite soft and I really enjoyed it. But he had a poker face and was a bit hard to read.

The next day I got an e-mail.

"Hi Jane. I just wanted to thank you for a great evening. It was wonderful to get to know you. I hope you had a nice time too. Victor."

P.S.: "I really enjoyed kissing you."

Over the next month, we saw one another regularly on weekends for dinner, movies, and such. There was no drama. There was no angst. No wondering if he was going to call back or if there would be another date. No begging to see him. He usually traveled Monday through Thursday and had told me that he was mine from midnight on Thursdays to midnight on Sundays when he would fly out again for the week. He had invited me to travel with him and said he would pay my ticket so we can spend the week together. We talked about doing things together that involved planning out a few months into the future. I was pretty sure he wasn't dating anyone else. He told me he had no interest in searching on Match and his subscription was about to expire. He was available. He was dependable. He stayed in constant communication. He was pretty normal. And I had no idea whatsoever to do with that. I began to wonder if it was too boring for me.

I felt like I was still searching for something ... something with more drama ... more excitement ... more *something*. What, exactly?

Victor was different — and that wasn't necessarily a bad thing — just something I wasn't used to. He wasn't in it for the conquest. I started wondering, "Have I become addicted to the search? Addicted to the thrill of the pursuit? Addicted to the disappointment and the rejection? Could I handle someone who was there for me? Would I see it as too boring or would I screw it up?" The only negative I could really see was he traveled a lot on business and was away Monday through Thursday so I could basically only see him on weekends.

Here was a man who pretty much did what I asked. He stayed in touch even when he was away. Spending New Year's Eve together seemed an assumption to him.

It was time to surrender to the fact I could have what I wanted. That I was deserving of a stable, sane man who was nice to me and treasured me. While I wasn't completely sure yet, I did find myself surfing less and less online. I lost interest in dating other people. But I also wasn't feeling the need to be with this man all of the time. Now that I had a man who was interested in being in a relationship — and also a full life of my own that didn't center around desperately needing a man — I behaved very differently.

One night, I was really tired and wanted a night alone. He completely understood. It's amazing how satisfying it feels to actually get what you want. I didn't know what the future held with Victor, but things felt quite different. I was sure we'd have our ups and downs and our differences as all relationships do, but I started to think I had a chance at real success.

My therapist found it interesting this man's name is Victor.

"Perhaps it's no coincidence it is very close to "victory," he said.

We shall see.

Is It Time To Stop Dating Online?

A few weeks before I met Victor, I had signed up for Match.com's "6-Month Dating Guarantee."

They were offering a guarantee that if I didn't meet someone special in six months, they would give me six months free. (I figured they probably owed me a few *years* for free after how much money I'd paid them.) In order to receive the guarantee, I had to sign up and follow their program rules. Basically, to e-mail five people each month, make sure my profile was visible, and have photos posted.

Victor and I had been dating two months, and since I wasn't interested in seeing anyone else, the only time I was on Match.com was to send off the five e-mails a month they require to keep my guarantee going. While I hoped I would never have to go back on there and use it, I had this nagging feeling inside if I let it lapse, something would happen with Victor and I would lose out and have to start my six months again from scratch.

While things weren't 100% perfect with Victor, they were pretty darn good. I actually had time for a life. To do things I wanted to do. It's truly amazing how much time this online dating thing can take up. It was refreshing to spend the time being in actual relationships … with a guy, with my friends and family, and with myself.

When I was going online to send out my five e-mails a month, I couldn't help but check out Victor's profile — particularly the part where it mentions when the person was last on the site. Every now and again I would see a note that said "active within the last 60 minutes" and it would piss me off royally.

This was a common problem for my online dating friends. We would be dating a man and could see right there they were still active online. Needless to say, we were, too, if we're in the position of seeing their profile is still active, but more often than not, we were only online to see what they are doing. (Yes, I realize this is a double standard!)

Victor and I had a conversation about it. I point blank asked him why he was still online. At first he said he only went online to respond to people who winked or sent him an e-mail so he could say, "No thank you." He said since he and I had started dating, he hadn't dated anyone else.

One day I get an e-mail from Victor. "Hey, do you know how to block someone on Match.com?"

"Why do you need to block someone?" I responded.

"Because I am constantly getting e-mails from Russian women who are looking for a U.S. husband."

"So why don't you just take your profile down?" I wrote.

"I'm not sure I'm ready for that, yet."

"Is there something missing in our relationship that makes you want to continue to search online for someone else?" I inquired hesitantly.

"No," he wrote.

"So why not take the profile down?"

"I don't have an answer for you. I guess I'm just not ready."

I was infuriated!

"What would you like me to do?" he asked.

I took a deep breath. "Well, in a perfect world I would want you to hide your profile. But I'm not going to tell you what to do. That has to be your choice."

About three weeks after that conversation, I noticed his profile had been taken down. When I saw his profile was "no longer available," at first it made me smile and then it scared the crap out of me. "Maybe this guy really likes me," I thought. But I got over it and took my profile down as well — for the first time since I began online dating oh so many years ago.

I was in brand new territory.

When It Rains, It Pours

They say when you least expect it, a man will show up.

It was a few days before Christmas. Victor and I had been dating for about a month, and I was in super-crazed holiday planning mode. I was still Christmas shopping, planning my menu for Christmas dinner, and running around like a chicken with its head cut off. In the midst of all the chaos, my dog, Sophie, had an appointment at the groomer, and so off we went.

Sophie is a bit of a diva dog. She is only 6 lbs. and I definitely pamper her like my child. She hates being in cages and I don't like to leave her anywhere if I don't have to, so I arranged for a private after-hours grooming session, as she absolutely hates to be groomed and cries and shakes the entire time.

I had been going to one particular grooming shop for a few months, and the same woman always groomed my dog. I had assumed she was the owner. But suddenly, there was a male groomer. It turned out he was her husband and was the actual owner of the shop. She had gone through a mid-life crisis and ended up leaving him — and the shop — behind. His name was Randy.

Randy was a very nice guy. He was 55 and in very good physical shape, although he had gray hair, was balding, and definitely looked his age (but he didn't really act it, which was great). So there we were chatting about the holidays and a multitude of things in general.

"All my friends keep telling me I need to start dating again, Jane," he said.

"That's probably a good idea," I said.

"But I haven't dated in 30 years. I wouldn't have a clue where to start."

"Well, you can always go online," I said.

There was a pause. "Are you married?" he asked.

"No."

"Would you like to go out to dinner with me one night?" he asked.

Here I was in unchartered territory. Not only was I getting asked out by a live person, which had virtually never happened in my life, but it was by a man who hadn't dated in 30 years. I didn't want to hurt his feelings when he was making great strides in getting back out in the dating world.

"Actually, I'm seeing someone," I said.

"Are you engaged?"

"No," I said.

"So what's the harm in dinner?" he asked.

"Sure! Why not?" I said.

It's important to point out here I couldn't have looked more like dreck if I tried. I was unshowered, with very little makeup, wearing an old pair of sweat pants and an old sweater. There were plenty of days when I was dressed to the nines and no one asked me out. Perhaps I was more approachable, more relaxed, or possibly just didn't care.

The funny thing was while I was somewhat attracted to this man, I was actually scared, too. I mean, if he was attracted to me in my "dreck" state ... that couldn't be good could it? But he wasn't going to reject me upon meeting me either, was he? That was a plus. So I bought myself some time and said I would go out with him after the holidays.

Two days after Christmas, I came home to find a message on my machine from Randy asking me out. The next day, my caller ID showed he called again. I was in a panic ... what to do, what to do? Did I dare go out with him while I was seeing Victor? Am I sabotaging myself with Victor by still seeking attention from men elsewhere? Or was I just so flattered by the fact someone finally asked me out in person and *not online* that I should just go for the experience? I also felt like I would be helping this guy out by going out with him when he hadn't had a date in 30 years. At least I knew that way his heart wouldn't get broken.

The next night, I was doing paperwork and the phone rang. I looked at the caller ID and it didn't register with me. I picked it up. It was him again. Persistent fellow, I will give him that. He asked me out for dinner. I hesitated for a minute and then said okay, but after New Year's. It was just to buy myself some more time. I still didn't know what to do.

Randy called after New Year's and I finally told him no. I wanted to see where things go with Victor.

A few weeks later, I was at a raw foods party a friend invited me to and a man started chatting with me and was with me the entire night. He was interesting — a life coach — and had a very positive, upbeat personality, but it was almost *too* positive. The cynic in me wondered about that.

I had told him I was writing a book about online dating and he told me he had done the online thing for quite awhile and had come to the realization he was simply not a monogamous person and he had to be really clear with the women he dated about that.

"Interesting," I thought, "he admits it up front."

Before he left the party, he stopped by to chat.

"So, Jane. Can I have your number?" he asked. "I'm attending a winery party tomorrow evening and I think you'd have a good time." The second live inquiry in a month!

Although I wasn't interested, I didn't want to embarrass him in front of the people we were with, so I said, "Sure. Here's my card." And we said good night.

He called the next day. "So what time is good for you tonight?"

"Actually, Lex, tonight is not good for me," I said.

"Okay, let's make it another time," he said, and we said our goodbyes.

He called one more time and left me a message. I called back and got his voicemail. "Hi Lex, it's Jane. I got your message and just wanted to be clear about things. I am seeing someone and I know you said you were not into monogamy. If you'd like to meet as friends, that's fine, but I'm really not interested in anything more."

He never called again and it was fine with me.

Life With Victor

Victor and I have been together for over a year now and life is really good.

For the first time in my life I am in a relationship free of drama, desperation, and disappointment. Our relationship is easy, fun, and fulfilling. I've found a really good guy who wants to be in a relationship, does what he says, shows up, and is emotionally healthy.

In the beginning, I was bothered by the fact Victor isn't a touchy/feely kind of person. He's not a hand-holder, a spooner, or a snuggler. At first I found it off-putting but then I realized I associated a man showing real affection with these physical acts. Then I looked back at some of the guys in my past who did do these things, but they didn't stay around for long, so I realized just because Victor didn't naturally grab my hand (I will grab his now), it doesn't mean he doesn't care about me. It's amazing how quickly you get over the stupid things that bother you in a relationship and focus on the more important stuff when it's the right person.

We have traveled together, cooked together, shopped together, and more. We like many of the same things and respect the other's interests even if they are not our own. He has become my best friend and I am completely in love with him.

It hasn't always been perfect and we've had our share of storms to weather — more to do with situations in life than with one another — and by caring, respecting, and communicating, we always come out in a better place.

Did eight years of online dating finally pay off? Would I have met Mr. Right if I hadn't dated online, but spent more time in bars, learning a male-oriented sport like golf, or gotten myself out there and been more social? Who knows?

What I do know is what changed was me. I learned to love myself. I learned to truly believe I deserved a great relationship. And I learned to create a full life for myself where the man in it didn't get 100% of my time and focus.

I realized a lot of my issues with men and my chasing after many of these unavailable men stemmed from my desire as a young child to get the attention of my father. He was a busy man with a full-time job and a side business so I had to pretty much follow him around and beg for his attention. I know now he didn't mean anything by it. He was doing the best he could in supporting our family and making a good living. But at the time, and for many years thereafter, deep down I thought to myself I wasn't worthy of a man's attention and I had to chase them down to get it. WRONG!

I also believed that men didn't stay around for very long and I had huge abandonment issues. And then one day my therapist pointed out to me what was right in front of me. My father — the first male that I ever had a relationship with in my life and who was undoubtedly the model for all my interactions with men — was currently taking care of my mother who was struggling with Alzheimer's. He was cooking for her, cleaning up after her, showering her, dressing her, and taking care of her every need in what is a very difficult and stressful situation. Everyone said he should put her away in a nursing home but he always insists he loves her too much and will stay by her side forever. Here Clyde was trying to show me that there is a man in my life who hasn't left. And as simplistic as that sounds, I came to the realization that not all men leave. The good ones stay around. My Dad did. And Victor did.

And when I think back on it, when I started to believe I was worthy of attention, I was lovable, and filled my life with a variety of activities so I wasn't dependent upon a man's attention, the right man showed up who gave me plenty of attention. Maybe I would have found him in the real dating world or maybe not. Online dating helped me to meet more men — and ultimately, the right one.

And They Lived Happily Ever After?

As I was trying to finish this book, I kept putting off writing this chapter. I didn't have an ending yet, did I? Victor and I aren't living together, engaged, or married. Now what do I do?

My wise therapist Clyde asked me, "Would it have made a difference?" Just because we might have taken that walk down the aisle wouldn't necessarily mean we would be together forever. It's funny how our culture conditions us to want to tie things up in a neat little package and have a Hollywood ending. But real life isn't like that, is it?

I did, however, recently receive a marriage proposal ... but it wasn't from Victor. Not so long ago, I was contacted by a certain garbage man who said he has been thinking about me a lot over the 14 months since we had broken up and he realized he wanted to marry me. To say I was shocked is an understatement.

Every woman dreams about getting a marriage proposal. I've dreamed of that day my entire life. But you don't really expect to get a marriage proposal from a man who broke up with you over a year ago when you are in a serious relationship with someone else!

I suppose it was the Cinderella part of me who always wanted to live "happily ever after" that was curious about this proposal and how it actually came to be.

"So, Justin" I began. "We've been apart for 14 months. How come you decided to propose marriage to me now?" I inquired.

"Well …" and there was a long pause. You have to realize whenever Justin was posed with a difficult question there was usually a long silence before one got an answer. And I quickly learned my usual technique of breaking up a difficult silence with some inane chit-chat was not the way to go with Justin. Difficult questions were often the most important ones and they required answers — no matter how long it took to actually get one.

I waited patiently through a long silence. "I've been thinking a lot about this, Jane, for the past few months," he began. "You know I recently turned 39, and I realized I don't want to be alone for the rest of my life."

"Uh-huh …"

"And it's hard to go out there and start a new relationship …"

"Uh-huh …"

"And I know you and Victor are getting serious and I know you wouldn't take me back if I didn't ask you to marry me …"

"And would you have asked me if I wasn't in a relationship with someone else?" I asked.

"Probably not."

I took all of this in and it hit me like a ton of bricks. Nowhere in his responses were "I love you, I can't live without you. I miss the hell out of you." It was pretty much all about him. And they were not good reasons to want to marry me. I couldn't believe how after years and years of desperately wanting a man to marry me, I was about to say no to a man who was proposing marriage.

The trouble was, this was the *wrong* man proposing marriage. Had he proposed 14 months ago, I probably would have said yes. But I knew better this time around. And I thank my lucky stars it didn't happen then because he would have been the wrong man for me.

Now I had someone who was a better fit for me. Someone who respected me, treated me well, and wanted to be with me. Someone who I felt was on the exact same page as I was.

"Sorry, Justin, no," I said.

He was incredulous. He couldn't believe I said no. "Jane, maybe you don't understand. I want you to bear my children," he said. Interesting.

"So, Justin, tell me," I inquired. "How come you broke up with me?"

"I don't really know," he said.

"So how do you know it won't happen again?" I said.

"Well, I believe in the sanctity of marriage, so if I commit to marriage, I would not run. I would stay and make it work," he replied.

"Even if you were miserable."

"I believe in marriage," he repeated.

"But clearly you were miserable when you were with me or you wouldn't have run. So what would be different this time around?" I said.

"We would be married," he said.

"But you may still be unhappy. You would live an unhappy life because you were married?" I said.

"You make it work because you are married," he said.

"If we ever got that far. I would never be sure you would show up at the church on the day of the wedding. You have a history of running, you know ..."

"That's not fair, Jane," he said.

"But it's true," I said.

"Can't you ever trust me again?"

"Actually, no. I trusted you four times. And you disappointed me four times. It took awhile, but I've finally learned my lesson."

The more I delved into his thought process the stranger it got. Suddenly he unleashed this angry torrent of emotions at me that I — and Clyde — hadn't forced him into couples therapy to make it work. This response from the man who didn't want to talk about it and had no reasons for why he ran when he broke up with me.

His rage continued and some interesting stuff came pouring out. I was too complacent. I didn't initiate sex enough. I wasn't enthusiastic enough. I wasn't playful enough.

For a woman who always had issues with "not being enough," this could have had serious consequences for me awhile back. But I knew I was good enough, thin enough, playful enough, pretty enough, and his barbs bounced right off me.

My turning him down brought up a wellspring of anger, hatred, and fury. Apparently nothing I had done in the relationship was right and it was clearly, in his opinion, my fault.

And yet he still wanted to marry me? This made absolutely no sense at all. We hung up, ending the conversation on a sour note. Day after day I received volatile e-mails from him — it was the most passionate I had seen him about anything. If only he'd been this passionate about doing something with his life, maybe we'd have gotten somewhere!

Justin's proposal was actually a blessing in disguise. It reinforced for me what I knew all along — I had a great guy in Victor. And while he may take a little while finding his way to wanting a serious long-term commitment, I know he will get there.

I am 45 years old and know there are no fairytale endings. But life is about the journey, and Victor and I are on a very happy and fulfilling one. I have finally met my match.

Addendum

Sage Advice From A Woman Who Has Been There

It seems I have inadvertently become quite the expert at online dating because of the sheer amount of years I have been doing it (eight), the number of guys I have dated (over 200), and the fact I have tried so many online dating sites (10).

So here is my advice — take from it what you will. These chapters were written at various times during my online dating escapades so you will ascertain different moods, but I believe there are some tips herein to either help you enter the online dating world or guide you through your existing foray.

I've asked my therapist, Clyde, to write the final chapter with his thoughts on online dating — quite a fascinating observation on his part.

Good luck and enjoy!

Online Dating Protocol

Online dating has its protocol like everything else.

First and foremost, I recommend you need to keep yourself safe — despite my own stupidity.

Never give out your home phone number to someone you really don't know well and *never* invite someone to your house on a first date (or let him or her pick you up). Always meet in a public place and make sure someone you know is aware of where you're going. There are just too many stories out there of stalkers, murderers, and online predators, so you really need to be careful.

At the end of every online date, I always offer to pay half of the bill. Most times, men will say no, but I believe they do appreciate the offer. But at times it's not appropriate to offer to split the check. For instance, I had one guy whom I met for an early dinner on a Sunday who drank quite a bit of alcohol (I really don't drink), then ordered a bunch of appetizers he mostly ate and then at the end of the date, he said, "Your half of the bill is ..." I couldn't believe it. I had an iced tea and nibbled on two bites of something!

I also recommend you don't meet someone without seeing his photo first. Granted, people do send older photos, but at least you get some idea what he looks like. I prefer to keep the surprises down to a minimum.

Beware of dating someone who is separated, because quite often they are not completely out of the relationship yet. I wouldn't date someone who is newly divorced either. I don't want to be "rebound girl."

You also need to be careful with people who have just moved to your area. More often than not, they are only looking for a tour guide to show them around.

Also, be on the lookout for weirdoes out there. I used to get e-mails from this guy who was a flight attendant and would fly into New York once or twice a week. He used to say he was looking for a place to stay whilst in New York and would give the woman who welcomed him to her house a lot of pleasure. I kid you not!

I'm also not a big fan of long distance online dating. I've pretty much decided an hour or less is a good cut-off. Otherwise, it becomes much too difficult to see the person. I've been contacted by people from Europe or California and let's be real, you aren't going to know if you hit it off until you meet one another in person and are you going to go to the expense of flying to meet someone for a first date just to realize you don't have chemistry? I've had enough bad first dates to realize a long distance one just isn't worth it. And this is particularly true because I have no plans to relocate — even for love!

Finally, and I know this is somewhat of a double standard, if a guy is in his late 40s or early 50s and he has NEVER been married, there is a commitment issue there. Granted, I know me and many of my friends are mid-40s and never married, but I have yet to run across a guy in his late 40s who has never been married who doesn't have issues about getting serious or settling down. We actually WANT to get married and settle down, that is the difference. I suppose we just haven't found the right guy yet.

Steer Clear Of Newbies

If I have learned one rule about online dating — well, in most cases, anyway — I would say one should steer clear of people who are new to online dating.

Why, you ask? Because most will be overwhelmed by the cyber-dating experience, feel like kids in a candy store like I did, and want to date around and get the most from their membership. Rarely will you find someone who has just tried online dating for the first time who will meet you and say, "You are it, and I don't want to date anyone else!"

I have always been someone who can't date more than one person at a time. After the first few dates, if I find I'm somewhat interested in someone, I feel like I owe it to myself and this person to just focus on him and see where it goes. I also feel like I am cheating on them by dating several people at once, which I realize is ridiculous if we aren't exclusive, but I guess that's just how I feel.

When I met "The Photographer," he had just joined Match. com and I believe I was his first or second date. I liked the fact he worked for a newspaper as a photographer because he had a journalistic background like me; however, he looked like he was a member of an '80s rock band with long hair and an earring. I didn't do long hair and earrings. I was more of the buttoned-up suit/executive type. But I figured I would venture out of my comfort zone.

He took me to a nice Italian restaurant in the theater district for dinner. We had a really good time over dinner and I figured I would give The Photographer a second shot. We caught up by phone a few days later and he said to me while he really liked me and we had a lot in common and hit it off, he had just joined Match.com and he wanted to date as many women as he could to really get the full experience of the cyber-dating world. I guess in some ways, I can't blame him.

Be Prepared For Some Bizarre Experiences

Sometimes in online dating you think you must be the only one who has bizarre experiences, but trust me, you're not alone. Bizarre is fairly routine.

I have one friend who was chatting with a guy online; they hadn't yet met, but I believe they had talked on the phone once or twice. One day she got a call from him and he had broken his foot and was in the hospital emergency room. He asked if she could come and be with him.

"Are you kidding?" she said. "We don't even know each other! You must have someone else you can call?" She hung up the phone completely bewildered. To him, she was already his girlfriend — and hence, his emergency contact.

This same woman had also met a man for Sunday brunch, and at the end when he asked if he could call her, she politely told him he was very nice, she had a nice time, but she didn't think they were a match.

He proceeded to yell and scream at her, "All you women are just in it for the free meals!"

Granted, I have met some men who've told me they meet women who brag to them they get a free dinner every night of the week by online dating.

Another man told me he corresponded with a woman for weeks and when he finally met her at the restaurant for dinner, she was in a wheelchair and had never told him she was a paraplegic! Just a minor detail, evidently.

A friend from New Jersey met a man from Connecticut online. They agreed to meet in upstate New York for dinner one Saturday night after hours and hours of talking online. Dinner went great. They kissed for quite awhile before saying goodbye. The next day she got an e-mail saying they live too far apart and it just won't work. Hello! You knew that *before* you met!

But I have to give this friend a lot of credit. She later went on a green singles dating web site and met someone who is 12 years her junior from Maine. She was divorced with two little kids. They talked and corresponded for nearly three months before they met. Four months later, he moved in with her. Today they are married and just bought a new house together and he is the greatest guy ever.

Online dating does produce results!

Beware The Conquistadors

There's a species of online daters I feel compelled to warn you about: "The Conquistadors".

How can you spot a Conquistador? There are a few telltale signs. First of all, the guy is *really* into you right away. You hit it off on the phone. In fact, you have a lot of opportunities to hit it off on the phone, because he calls you three or four times a day. You may even start talking about how hot it's going to be when you first meet. You're both counting the minutes until your first get-together. He is so energized and into you. You are so excited and flattered! Finally, you have a chance to meet a guy who isn't playing hard to get and is being out there with his feelings. I have one word for you: RUN!

This type of man is totally in it for the conquest. He comes on really strong and very intense. He sweeps you off your feet and makes you think this will be the love of your life. He can't wait to see you … can't wait to be with you, and does nothing but think of you. And once he has you, he's gone.

I've dated quite a few Conquistadors in my time, and their MO is always the same. They are constantly calling me … just to say hi … because they were thinking of me … because they are counting the minutes until they see me. If you take a step back, you will see their energy is almost frenetic. There is really no sound reason why they would be so into you when they haven't even met you — or maybe you have met for a quick coffee and are now planning a real date and they just can't wait.

Jack was my last Conquistador. We met on eHarmony. He wanted to "Fast Track" which means you don't go through all of the pre-ordained steps eHarmony makes you go through to get to know one another but instead start exchanging open e-mails right away. We met for coffee at the local Starbucks and he was quite the charmer. We talked for a few hours about our likes and dislikes, jobs and hobbies. He was a mortgage broker and loved to work out every day. I told him I was just getting into working out. When he walked me to my car, he started kissing me and I have to say my knees did go weak. It was cold out and I finally said I had to go. He called within minutes after I arrived home.

"Hi. How are you?" this sexy voice responded when I answered the phone.

"Good. And you?" I said.

"I'm great. Can you believe that connection we had? It was amazing."

"Mmmmm. It was nice," I said.

"What are you doing Thursday night? I'd like to take you to dinner," he said.

"Wow," I thought, "that was one of the fastest requests for a second date I've had." (Keep in mind this was before Victor.)

"Sure, that would be nice," I said.

"Great. I'll call you and we can set a time and place. Have a great night. I'm still thinking about kissing you ..."

As it turned out, Jack was leaving the next day for a conference in Atlantic City. I don't know about most people, but when I am away on a business trip, I am busy. He invited me to join him, and at first I thought he was kidding, but he was serious. Naturally, I declined (Yes, I finally did learn my lesson.) He called me while he was driving there. He called me when he arrived there. He called me before he went to dinner. He called me after dinner and before he went to go play Blackjack. That should have been my first clue his energy was frenetic. Sure, I had an inkling maybe he was all about the conquest, but I wanted to believe this one would be different ... I shouldn't be so jaded and cynical I might miss the love of my life.

The constant calling kept up until Thursday, when he insisted he had to pick me up because he was "old school." I was hesitant to let him come to my house, but he was very persistent and finally wore down all of my arguments.

When he arrived, he kissed me right away ... a long kiss that made me weak in the knees again. He took me to a romantic restaurant and when he got up to go to the men's room, he leaned over and kissed me on the cheek as he passed by. He held my hand as we headed toward the car. All of these romantic gestures made me feel quite sexy and cared for and desired.

I have to admit I was incredibly turned on by his attention, and really wanted this guy. And I had a choice. I could wait it out to see what happened or I could sleep with him right away and see what his story was. If he was interested in a relationship, I would find out right away, and if he was just interested in the conquest, it would be obvious as well.

So we came back to my house and he helped me off with my coat. Before I could close the closet door and turn around he grabbed me in his arms and we began kissing. We kissed for a really long time so I finally invited him upstairs where clothes began flying off within minutes.

I have to say for a guy who worked out constantly, I was not very impressed by his body. And his lovemaking skills were incredibly mechanical. When he left, I expected a call because that was what he did. He called all the time. But for the first time since he came into my life, my phone didn't ring.

There was no call the next day either, so in the early afternoon I sent him a playful message just saying, "Hey sexy, how are you?" He responded by saying he didn't want to pursue this relationship any further because he thought we were too different — in particular that exercise and being athletic weren't as high on my priority list as they were on his. (Um … hello … you knew this *before* we slept together.)

He then called me, wanting to explain his side of it. I told him he was only in it for the conquest and he was the ultimate player. He adamantly disagreed.

"So then why did you sleep with me when you knew I wasn't into exercising as much as you?" No answer.

"But I still want us to be friends," he kept replying.

"With friends like you, who needs enemies?" I said, and hung up.

He showed his hand — a Conquistador. And while I was upset and pissed off, I was glad I just let it go and found out early on the kind of man he was instead of wasting my time.

No matter how much your heart may be telling you the frenetic guy who calls you 10 times a day is different and how flattered you feel he really wants you, run, don't walk, the other way!

Really
– It's Not Just Me

A friend called me one morning and told me to turn on *Dr. Keith*. I had never seen this daytime talk show before, but apparently it focuses on a psychiatrist like Dr. Phil. This episode featured guests talking about online dating. After seeing these individuals, I am happy to report I am not quite as insane as some cyber-daters are!

One woman said she had met over 100 men and the longest she ever dated any man online was two dates! That seems pretty unbelievable. Then they showed a tape of one of her first dates and I could see why.

She showed up on her date with her little white dog. Now, I have a little white dog, but I would never show up on a first date with her (unless we were going to a dog park, I suppose). She forced this poor man to say hello to her dog. Then she proceeded to grill her date on whether he really was 35, if he was really 5' 9", and so on. When he said he was actually only 5' 8.5" she screamed at him, "You lied!" Okay, get a grip. There are worse things in life to lie about.

Another guest on the show was a man who had dated over 700 women and actually kept a spreadsheet on each one! He noted which was good for a "booty call," for instance. At least he admitted to being a serial dater.

You Are What You Advertise

As someone involved in advertising and public relations, I suppose I have an advantage when it comes to posting an online dating ad — or at least evaluating them. You have to know your product, know what the marketplace wants, and promote it well.

If anything, I think I have a good opinion of what does and does not work. Take, for instance, the guy who advertises in the second line of his profile he is "great in the sack." Come on ... do you really need to state this? When someone needs to so blatantly characterize themselves as something — creative, nice, smart, etc. — they usually *aren't*.

Men online seem to be afflicted with two common traits. The first is when it comes to describing themselves, nine out of 10 male profiles will say "my friends describe me as ...". Who cares what your friends say? How do *you* describe yourself?

The second scenario is guys will *always* say, I'm 46 but really look 36. Or I'm 46 but act 36. Or I'm 46 but feel 36. Come on!

Act your age! Who cares how old you are? Apparently the age issue is more important to them than to us. Moreover, most 46-year-old guys don't want to date a 46-year-old woman. What's up with that? Do they honestly think if they are dating a 28-year-old woman they will look younger by association? I think not! If anything, it will only make their age more obvious!

There are the men online who profess to be former models and will blatantly tell you they only want model looks in the women they date. Guys who report they will only respond if you have a recent, head-to-toe photo, and ones who seek "no drama."

My all-time favorite is the man who says he has "no baggage" and doesn't want the woman he dates to have any either. Okay, how out of touch is he with himself? There is no one on this planet who doesn't have relationship baggage. And I mean no one.

Then there are the ones who are wearing a baseball cap in every photo. Um, I think we can figure out there's a hair problem going on. And what's up with the guys who pose in sunglasses? I want to see someone's eyes. They truly are the mirrors to someone's soul.

I don't understand how people who don't post a photo and don't take the time to fill out a profile expect to get any responses. Then there are the people who hide their profile so while they can read about you and check you out and like what they see enough to wink or write you, they can't understand why you don't want to converse back with them or meet them. These are the people I suspect are married or doing something they shouldn't be doing!

A Great Cure For Loneliness

I know there are plenty of us online who aren't actually into the dating part, but we simply want to make a connection with another human being — especially on a cold, dark, lonely Saturday night. And so we surf the Internet, wink at people, e-mail people, IM people — without any intention of actually meeting.

There were times when I was in a relationship and still surfed the online dating sites. You're home on a Saturday night. You're lonely. Or you want to see if there is anyone better out there. Let's be real. Everybody does it. (They just don't do it in front of you, like Mike!)

I think a lot of us also search online to make ourselves feel like we're doing something about dating and moving past an old relationship or a bad breakup, but in reality, all we are actually doing is looking or flirting. And after years and years of online dating I cannot believe I still got nervous when meeting a new man. I wasn't sure I was ready to put myself out there again. To put up with the rejection again. To sift through man after man who is not sure of what he wants, isn't ready to settle down, or is just looking for sex.

Dating is hard. Dating is horrible. I was so sick of first dates. I feel like I'm on a job interview every time I have a first date. And after having more than 200 first dates, I am — to put it bluntly — sick of myself. I'm sick of hearing me talk about myself. And more importantly, sometimes I'm sick of hearing guys talking on and on about themselves, and never taking a break to ask me anything about me. I know this sounds silly, or maybe even ridiculous, but some nights, I would really just rather sit on the couch, snuggle with my Maltese, Sophie, and watch a movie. I don't need to take a shower, shave (*everywhere*), put on makeup, blow dry my hair, and find something sexy to wear. Some nights, it's just not worth all of the effort. (And do guys really appreciate it anyway?) Cynical, but true.

I can't tell you how much trouble I have gone to in order to pick out just the right lingerie to wear for a boyfriend only to have him prefer it was off. He couldn't have cared less what color it was, how much lace was on it, or how much fabric wasn't there. He just wanted to get to what was underneath.

So why did I continue to bother? Sometimes I asked myself that. I had to bother because I wanted a relationship. And while I am someone who absolutely abhors process, I can't pick a man out of a catalogue to marry. I have to go on a first date with him, and then a second date, and so on. But at times, I hated dating so much I found every excuse to find something wrong with every man who contacted me. Too old. Too young. Doesn't make enough money. Has too many kids. Lives too far away. Too attractive. (Yes,

I actually think some men are too attractive for me. It intimidates the hell out of me!)

At one point, I decided maybe this online dating thing wasn't working. I've tried going to church (I'm really not into organized religion), taking classes (all female or gay men, every time), or contacting local singles organizations. At the time, I was actually *too young* for all of the ones in my area — sometimes you just can't win! One of the only things I hadn't tried was a matchmaking service.

A friend told me her daughter met her husband through one of these services. I knew they were pricey and that was always one of the reasons I didn't pursue them. But I started to do some inquiries. It was a bit intimidating, as first they would have to approve me to make sure I was attractive enough for them to find a suitable match. And then, of course, I would have to pay for the service. I found out it could range anywhere from $2,500 to $5,000 and above depending upon how picky I chose to be.

While I was desperate at times and did want a mate, I just couldn't see paying $5,000 for someone to introduce me to my Mr. Right. And there was no guarantee! And how is someone else going to know who my soul mate is?

The Profile

Despite best intentions, you really can't trust someone's online profile.

I know, I know — in online dating, pretty much the only thing you have to go on is the profile. But in my years of online dating — and the fact I now have some perspective — I've come to learn most people's profiles are dead wrong.

Think about it. How many people *really* know themselves? And if they do, are they really going to put all of their issues and negatives out there for the world to see?

An online dating profile is a place where someone creates the perfect them. It's the person they have always wanted to be. They can be whomever and whatever they want to be.

The other day, my friend read me a few profiles from men she was corresponding with. After three or four, they all started to sound the same. Even worse, they didn't really *say* anything.

Case in point is Victor. His profile said he traveled "occasionally" on business and liked it, and he was one of the few people his friends knew who actually liked his job.

As Victor and I got to know one another, I found out he traveled practically all the time and he didn't really like his job. Thankfully, those were just minor things that were incorrect on his profile and he was really a great guy who actually wanted to be in relationship.

A man — or a woman for that matter — isn't going to say in their profile they are needy. They have abandonment issues. They are actually very insecure. They need their space and want to date around. They are actually unemployed, still married, or living with Mom and Dad. That's not very attractive is it?

I suppose the old adage is true — let the buyer beware!

Kids ... Or No Kids?
That Is The Question

When you are dating, one of the big questions that inevitably comes up is whether or not you want kids.

You may think it's a bit too early to worry about that when you're just trying to find someone to date, but actually it's never too early. When you are over 30, one should be pretty clear about whether he or she wants kids or not, because it does make a big difference.

If you had asked me in my twenties, I would have said I definitely didn't want kids. In my thirties, I wavered, and then I was sure that yes, I definitely wanted kids. No question about it! As I approached my forties, I wasn't sure again, but knew if I did have them, I could only do so if the father was 50% involved at all times and didn't expect me to do the bulk of the child rearing.

And then came Sophie, and my perspective changed. For 42 years, I'd been coming and going as I pleased. If I wanted to stay out for hours at a time I could do that. If I wanted to pick up and spontaneously go away for the weekend or go stay over someone's house, I could do that. Not with a dog. Nor with a child, for that matter.

While I absolutely love Sophie, I struggle with a bit of resentment over my loss of freedom. I can only be away from the house about six hours at the most. If I want to go into the city or go away for the weekend, I need to find someone to watch her. I will never put her in a kennel, so my dog-sitting choices are a bit limited. Thank goodness my parents love Sophie and will watch her nearly any time I want. But she has changed my perspective about having kids.

My neighbors are single mothers. They can't just pick up and go to the movies or dinner with me whenever they want. They have to make sure their ex-husbands or a babysitter can watch them. They can't leave them home alone for six hours to go shopping like I do with Sophie. They can't just pick up and travel whenever they want to.

I see them running their kids around to gymnastics, soccer practice, and ballet. My neighbor told me it has been years since she has just sat at the beach and read a book — usually she is throwing her son in the waves or building sandcastles. I accompanied my neighbor to her son's science fair and almost died of culture shock at the din in the auditorium as hundreds of 10-year-olds ran around from booth to booth.

Now I'm in my mid-40s, I don't think I want children. I don't think I have it left in me to be so selfless I can just give up everything for a child. And as I peruse all of the profiles of divorced men who have kids and I read their statements which remark their kids will always come first in their life, I start to think, "You know, *I* want to come first in a man's life." I don't want to be second to his child. And I don't want to start going to soccer practice, ballet, or gymnastics. If a man has grown children, that's one thing, but if he has little kids, he's not for me.

Be clear about whether or not you want kids now — because it *will* cause problems later on.

Would I Do It Again?

Despite everything I have written here, I would definitely date online again should the need arise — which I hope it doesn't!

Online dating has its good and bad points. The best thing about it, as my friend Liz first told me, is it widens the net and puts you in touch with people you would probably have never met otherwise.

Every time I think about the fact Victor lives in an apartment complex I passed on a weekly basis for two years, it amazes me. I probably passed him in Starbucks or Dunkin' Donuts or Barnes & Noble but would have never known he was available (maybe all of us single people should wear little nametags or badges saying "I'm available"). Match.com brought us together and for that I am grateful — despite the eight or so years of online dating experiences, ups and downs, weirdoes, commitment phobes, and, of course, conquistadors.

I did ask him recently how he found his way to Match.com. He said he saw a television commercial for the service and thought he would give it a try.

Over the years, I lost touch with my friend Liz who got me into online dating. I was curious to see how she was doing and if she was still married, so I contacted her. I'm happy to report she is still married, and happily at that! Good going, Liz.

It's also funny that I was someone who said men never approached me in everyday life and asked me out, but ever since I met Victor, it's been happening more and more. So I guess I would say to be open, positive, and not desperate. Just go about your life. Date online. Date offline. Keep your options open. And be really clear about the type of person you want. I don't mean hair color, eye color, height and weight. I mean know the type of person you want.

Without a doubt, I definitely think online dating is a venue where people who want to meet people gather. Just beware. Be smart. And don't take it so seriously. It also doesn't hurt if you truly believe you deserve a great person in your life. When I finally gave up the belief relationships were hard, there wasn't a man out there for me, and men always leave me, the right man showed up. I suppose it also didn't hurt I learned to love myself just the way I am.

V is indeed for victory!

A Professional Opinion

For a final thought, I decided to let a professional take over and offer an expert opinion. Here's what my therapist, Clyde Baldo, M.A., had to say about online dating:

"People are very attracted to online dating. In fact, many people are addicted to online dating. In a world built on fairy tales — especially in this case — Cinderella or the white knight — people get to live out the excitement of that ideal relationship. The problems lie in the fact it is not a real relationship but one in cyberspace, filled with false images, predatory agendas, and compulsive desires. Online dating fills the void of loneliness. Ironically, it ends up exacerbating the void to the point of having to get back online to medicate that pain and disappointment. That is the definition of addiction. No difference if it's love, sex, or scotch. You always need the next one.

In a world of over-stimulation and the need to collect, the online "shopper" gets to fill his or her closet. The excitement of getting that e-mail message feels real, the upset of not hearing back from Mr. Right feels real, the anger over being rejected by Ms. Perfect feels real, but in truth it is a subconscious playground to play out one's deepest wounds and often is a tool for psychological masochism.

So the solution becomes to create profiles of one's alter ego so one can experience who he or she wants to be in their ideal perception that would lead to "happiness." Lying, deception, and false interactions ensue so one can capture the energy of the other. It's a brilliant game of chess, but one that always ends in a stalemate — no pun intended.

For men, the temptation to seduce, conquer, and enjoy many women becomes very intoxicating. There are way too many choices — meaning there is always someone better, always an escape clause. Online dating usually doesn't lead to relating, sharing, togetherness, but fast food online shopping for hedonistic pleasures and psychological manipulations.

Relationships don't happen from checklists, or heights and weights — they happen in real time by being in each other's energy and experiencing what happens. There is definitely a percentage of people doing it that way. But most become serial e-mailers — hiding behind false images they can't maintain in person. So many people have said, "It was so great over the computer; we really seemed to gel and also over the phone but in person it was just the opposite — dead, flat, weird, boring."

There are serial daters — people just going from one date to the other under the illusion of intimacy or the delusion of wanting a relationship. They don't. They just want to feel wanted and busy. And are usually bitter, lonely, and very scared.

Online dating becomes a bakery to the diabetic. A bar to the alcoholic. It is way too intoxicating and way too safe in its anonymity to play out one's pathology.

People are very linear. They believe what one writes in their profile is true and that is who they are. Sometimes for the evolved person it is very close to true but for most, it is who they want to present and who they feel protects them from their own judgment and gives them the best chance of "landing the fish."

It is strategized, concocted, and not real. Guys can play James Bond and women can be Madonna. Guys can be Albert Einstein and women can be Susan Sarandon. Just package it correctly and sell it to the market looking for that product.

So people are greatly disappointed and let down by the reality of who they have spent months intriguing with, fantasizing about, flirting with. They usually are left with nothing but the next profile. It is a perfect drink in this addicted world to being responded to and wanting to feel attractive. You don't even have to leave the house. But when you do, you discover your life is barren, not congruent to the persona created in cyberspace and full of disconnection.

Online dating in its pure form is a wonderful opportunity to meet new people and find someone wonderful — either as a partner or a friend — but unfortunately, in a world filled with desperation and addiction, it keeps the love and sex junkie enslaved."